Elementary school drawing class, c.1898
Photograph courtesy of E.J. Milton Smith ATD FSAE

Published by Jeremy Mills Publishing Limited
on behalf of Leeds College of Art and Design

www.jeremymillspublishing.co.uk

First published in 2008

ISBN 978–1–906600–35–8

Printed on 130gsm Cycluset – 100% recylced paper

Do it 100%

DESIGN
PEDAGOGY
RESEARCH

LEEDS EDITED
2007 BY KATE
HATTON

Contents

Acknowledgements

I would like to thank the following people whose interest provided valuable support for the 2007 conference, notably in its initial stages of development. These include, in particular, Guy Julier and Derek Horton from Leeds Metropolitan University whose discussions in the autumn of 2006 helped me to make sense of the design research possibilities from the original conference idea and to establish a Leeds based focus, and Claire O'Mahony who encouraged me in an application for funding from the Design History Society.

Members of staff at Leeds College of Art and Design who devoted time and interest to the project such as Christian Lloyd, Simone Goodwill, Garry Barker, Kate Conlon and Chris Graham and also the students whose work and ideas contributed much to the scope of the research.

Conference contributors whose papers do not appear in this text, but whose research was an important part of the conference's success: James Fathers, Tim Benton, Teal Triggs, Kirsten Hardie, Christopher Bamford, Margo Blythman, Bernadette Blair and Susan Orr.

Finally, I'd like to thank Hazel Goodes and Sharon Emery for their unstinting patience with the updating of texts and the proof reading.

Kate Hatton

Foreword

Kate Hatton

This publication came from an idea for a conference on pedagogy I instigated at Leeds College of Art and Design in 2007. The aim of the conference was to explore the shifting perspectives of design and pedagogy research and their locations within contemporary art and design education. My vision was to promote the idea of a regular meeting of minds within art and design teaching and to situate new and developing forms of research within an art and design setting. The 2007 conference was jointly funded by the Design History Society, Leeds Metropolitan University and Leeds College of Art and Design. I had the idea for a conference after finding little available material on more recent design education based research, whilst at the same time knowing there must be many kinds of research going on in various institutions involving local action research and case studies of pedagogic practices. It seemed to me that all people probably needed was a focus and an opportunity to get together to talk about art and design pedagogy and to disseminate their research findings.

The call for papers for the 2007 conference elicited a wide response from design theorists, historians and design researchers in education who originated ideas from their own research practice. They came to Leeds to introduce their ideas through talks and workshops around the three main conference themes, which were: *Design Practice and Pedagogy*, *Design History and Pedagogy* and *Perspectives on Design and Pedagogy*. The speakers were chosen for their positions as contemporary theorists on design and design education or practitioners within the field of design pedagogy, namely tutors of design practice and design history, although the emphasis intended by the conference's main dialogue was around the interdisciplinary nature of design thinking within art and design education and recent forms of research.

Not all papers from the original conference are represented here, although ten out of the fourteen pieces are. They are mostly reproduced in their original format or, on occasion, slightly updated versions were provided, rather than working to a more prescriptive formula. Therefore, a sense of the variety of material offered at the conference and the flavours of the original dialogues and discussions are hopefully kept mostly intact. Minor amendments have only been made through further reflection to bring the papers together for publication. I hope those represented here give a sense of the direction this conference took and its primary aim, which was to begin a dialogue around design pedagogy and design thinking in the early twenty-first century and set an agenda for new forms of research.

Major shifts have occurred in design pedagogy since the nineteenth century, when the Design Schools established by government to train designers for industry were a major focus for design pedagogy. Those institutions established in cities such as Leeds, Bradford, Manchester and Birmingham were an important part of design pedagogy's industrial history. In the twentieth century, design courses, run as part of the DipAD programmes, began to promote design as more of a disciplinary practice alongside art. The Bauhaus model of art and design education was incorporated into Foundation and BA programmes, serving as a diagnostic focus for the development of design skills and design thinking. Art schools, such as the Leeds model in the 1960s and 1970s, also developed curriculum practices that signified a holistic approach to design practice and theory, whereby solutions to a design problem could be considered concurrently in both technical and artistic terms within the same design briefs.

More recently, undergraduate and postgraduate design education may have become reflective of the 'postmodern' design industries, particularly in the 1980s and 1990s and this trend was supported both by rapidly developing design cultures and design histories, which promoted a concept of design that was more far reaching than the 'heavy industry' approaches of British design's past heritage. Individualistic designs, rather than mass produced wares, formed the basis of design production and design consumption. New questions could now be asked around design practice, design history and even the role of the designer as a contemporary theorist who contemplates, perhaps more readily, questions around consumption, globalisation and diversity. To put this more simply, there had been a growing awareness since the 1990s of the designer's role within a global environment and, within more recent contexts of learning and pedagogic research, there are clearly developing notions being made by design practitioners, theorists and researchers about how design pedagogy may prepare the undergraduate and postgraduate student for global and sustainable design development.

Keeping up to date with such trends as these, the 2007 conference tackled questions about what and whom design pedagogy now serves. The papers delivered were on various design-related ideas but they all referenced the context of contemporary design pedagogy. Gen Doy discussed the idea of pedagogy and consumption, and the interdisciplinary nature of design and cultural displacement. Using the analogy of 'shoplifting' to explore the complex arena of design education against patterns of consumption, she also showed how design and pedagogy may be examined within pedagogic and philosophical contexts, raising significant questions around design teaching and learning and what students, as 'consumers', may derive from this. Peter Oakley analysed the hidden power within practical activities through the concept of 'praxeological subjectification' which refers to how creative design ideas may be stimulated by practical activity. He uses cultural and post-structural theories to analyse his observations of design workshop activities and provides an original critique of the symbolic experiences of design students in design education. The keynote address of the conference was by Professor Guy Julier, and focused on 'Practising Design Culture' in which he emphasised the dramatic changes made to the meanings and practices of design over the last fifteen years and how design's pedagogy might have demonstrated such changes. This paper called for more reflective designers and a design pedagogy that might communicate social, cultural, environmental, political and symbolic values. Tara Winters' paper dealt with the idea of how design pedagogies reflect transformative learning and signalled how design research might enable this process. Her case study of a research based design degree programme at the Elam School of Fine Arts, a part of the University of Auckland in New Zealand, reflected how design pedagogy research stretches across the globe.

The Leeds College of Art and Design Research Group

I would like to extend a special tribute to members of the Research Group at Leeds College of Art and Design, whose own research for the conference was developed around many constraints, particularly of time and finances. When we began to work towards the idea of a conference, many Leeds staff were fledgling researchers. This was often only because we hadn't had sufficient time to explore design research ideas outside work due to heavy teaching loads and the numerous responsibilities associated with large student groups. As yet the college does not benefit from an HEI research budget but perhaps this will come soon, hopefully, in the near future. Nonetheless, researchers such as Samantha Broadhead, David Collins, Sherelene Cuffe, Karen Dennis, Janine Sykes, Eleni Tracada and myself, attempted to put together papers that dealt with what we felt were significant issues in design pedagogy, sometimes emanating from early held passions about our own design education, particularly from our experiences as students and tutors. The knowledge developed from this source has provided a rich form of research, which embedded the realities of student and tutor experiences within the context of an exciting and distinctive design pedagogy research culture.

Finally, what might research into design and pedagogy mean in twenty years time? Hopefully, there will be many more publications like this one, which are based on people getting together to discuss their ideas. Whether the design subject fields have new names, such as 'material culture', or other such shifts in emphasis, does not really matter. What matters is that people carry on researching design pedagogy and reflecting on their own experiences and practices in order to establish a studied and appropriate design pedagogy research environment for the future.

Kate Hatton
Leeds, May 2008

Design • Pedagogy • Research

Chapter 1

Practising Design Culture:
Notes on the Alignment of Complexity and Pedagogy

Guy Julier
Leeds Metropolitan University

Introduction

Just as the meanings and practices of design have changed dramatically over the past fifteen years, so should have its pedagogy. This essay begins anecdotally, drawing on my experience of teaching design at Leeds Metropolitan University.

In 1991 I acquired a set of shelves. These were from an annual auction of prototypes produced by graduating three-dimensional design students at the then-called Leeds Polytechnic. They are telling of their era: very post-Memphis, large, concerned ostensibly with technical problem-solving toward aesthetic effect. They speak of a time when the workshop, making and design as embodied in the object prevailed.

Compare this example with a sample of final design projects produced in the last two years at the same (but now very different) institution: a learning system for understanding the recyclability of different plastics for primary school children; a baseball cap for avoiding recognition by surveillance cameras; a hoodie for autistic teenagers; an office trolley for hot-desking not-very-committed employees; an ashtray for lovers; a designer self-harming kit; specialised tableware for eating with hands in a posh restaurant.

The 1991 piece signals a sensibility that places 'good design' on the aesthetic and technical resolution of the object. The object itself sits within a specific historical canon of design pedagogy. Storage or shelving joined the chair and the teapot as stock design exercises of the twentieth century, promoted by Gropius, Eames, Propst, Sottsass and many other heroes of modernism and postmodernism. This wasn't the only kind of design happening in Leeds 1991, but it certainly occupied a more dominant role than today.

The students of the classes of 2005–7 display a different sensibility. A key word in their project descriptors is 'for'. Eschewing alienated objects for ease of exhibition, they are seeking connectivity with real or imagined publics. The measure of design success, of good design, is not just callibrated by aesthetic impact or technical resolution but by the extent that the object may adjust or facilitate new behaviours and sensibilities. The objects and contexts that they intervene in are more varied. They are disembodied from the historical canons and hierarchies of what legitimates design intervention and are more concerned with content than form. In other words, for today's students, design culture, these days, is a much more open game.

So what has happened between 1991 and today that might have changed the panaroma within which design students study? Here are just a few examples in alphabetical order: A levels in Design and Technology (Resistant Materials, Textiles, Product) in the UK, and similar educational developments elsewhere; branding becoming more central to organisations; TV design 'makeover' shows; closure of some undergraduate design history courses; creative industries policy and analysis within government; creative quarters within urban planning critical design; design festivals; digitization; Droog Design; *Icon* magazine; Ikea; Rapid Prototyping; transformation design; Visual Culture Studies; Wayne Hemingway.

The following trends may be extracted from this list: design and creativity is placed more central to government policy in terms of economic, cultural and educational policies; there has been subversion of hierarchies within and the blurring of edges of design practice; there has been a massification of 'knowing consumer' engagement with design and some of its processes combined with the narrowing or dissolution of the cultural and temporal spaces between its production and consumption.

This essay takes each of these tendencies in turn. The first, then, relates to the institutional, ideological and policy environments of design pedagogy in the recent past. The second draws attention to the shifting ground on which design is carried out in the profession and the challenges this lays down for design pedagogy. The third focuses on the social and cultural world of design consumption. Each of these is characterised by binary opposites that reveal the complexity within which design pedagogy is placed.

Educational Policy and Political Economy

A brief glance through the history of design education suggests that it has always harboured self-problematising discussion. This runs through, for example, Lethaby's rejection of the term 'dessinateur' in favour of 'industrial artist' during his directorship of Central St Martin's in 1912. The former suggested that the designer would be a technician, the early twentieth century version of a mouse monkey. The latter suggested, perhaps, a more elevated, intellectually driven professional status. Equally, the frequent schisms at the Bauhaus during the 1920s or the Ulm Hochschule für Gelstatung in the 1960s or at the Eina school in Barcelona in the 1970s mostly all revolved around a struggle for definition. Should design pedagogy be oriented as a vocationally driven activity, toward industry, or does it engage a more humanities-driven approach that welcomes critique and experimentation?

These questions come at a time of intense discussion in the UK as to the future of design education. In 2007, Imperial College, London, funded by the Audi Foundation released its report on design education, 'Making the most of design excellence: equipping UK designers to succeed in the global economy'. In the United States, the Design Studies Forum has instigated a debate as to the role that historical and theoretical studies in design has within the wider college campus. Also in 2007, the UK's Cultural and Creative Skills, a Sector Skills Council licensed to the Secretary of State for Education and Skills, made a bid for greater regulation of design training. It proposed kite-marking design courses by specifying distinct skills attainment in order for them to be able to apparently 'successfully operate' in the design industry. The ensuing debate – in which the Design Council was vigorously engaged – led to the UK Design Industry Skills Development Plan (Design Skills Advisory Panel, 2007).

Ironically, the attention given in government policy circles to design since 1997 has come at a time of decreased economic performance of the sector in the UK. According to the latest British Design

Valuation Survey (British Design Innovation, 2006), while fee income made by the design industry has dropped markedly since 2001, the actual numbers of designers and design firms practising has not changed significantly. Its conclusions are that savings made by designers through, for example, increased technological efficiency or quicker turnaround of projects are being passed on to clients. Designers, in other words, are being more productive for the same money. Designers retain or chase clients by keeping their prices keen or by throwing in added extras. Design consultancies are ever trying to trim their sails to provide more efficient workflows, so their marketing budgets and strategies are increasingly important in the bid to maintain recognition.

Ten years ago, product designer Geoff Hollington suggested, in the context of increasing multisciplinarity and teamworking of designers, that Philippe Starck may be the last great 'Designer Hero'. The era of the individual star designer is over, he argued (Hollington 1998). The emphasis on the individual 'creative', within the format of the design consultancy, appears to live on, however. They are still highly dependent on possessing named, recognised designers within their ranks in order to attract and retain clients. It is the 'creative' who does the project presentation to clients, who the client refers to most commonly, and who acts as the mediator of value.[1]

In support of this process, educational policy supports the fashioning of the creative individual. Angela McRobbie (2007) talks of the 'Los Angelisation of London' (or it could be of Leeds, Luton or Lincoln) that bears all the hallmarks of the Blair period. Blair's 'go it alone' agenda is mirrored in the creative economy, she argues. This is:

> ... bound up with deeper social transformations which involve redefining notions of selfhood and which encourage more expansive forms of self reliance. These new more flexible forms of selfhood are institutionally grounded in education and through pedagogical styles as well as the transformation of the curriculum.

By the latter, one would include the development of Records of Achievement and Professional Development Portfolios. The ethic of 'self-reliance' (itself also embedded in Chris Smith's *Creative Britain* thesis), corresponds, 'with styles of working on a project-by-project basis'. Thus, by extension, design education neatly fits in with a wider political agenda of selfhood, wherein more flexible approaches to labour are promoted.

The self is also imbricated into a promotional culture in McRobbie's terms. She goes on to identify the importance of the 'single big hit' that the design graduate aims for: the attention grabbing, media recognisable creative outcome that will work for personal launching. Hence, typically, the design graduate will offset the drudgery of a routine job, such as working as a mouse monkey, while that one personal project is developed that will buy them the big break and release from that routine.

McRobbie's thesis could be criticised for romanticising the very systems she is critiquing. Her imagined young creative is not the only version. But the myth of being a designer as a creative individual is also bolstered by the realities of the system of design consultancies, by educational policy and not least by the design media.

The cultivation of selfhood and authorial voice is also a necessary component in order to maintain designer value and the cache of the creative. The concentration on personality and personal style is a more traditional element of the art school tradition (see, in particular, Frith and Horne 1987). Following McRobbie's argument, its instrumentalisation toward certain objectives within political

---

1. This issue has emerged strongly within the 'Counting Creativity: Understanding the Systemization of Design Practices' Arts and Humanities Research Council, Workshop Network, 2006–7, AH/E508332/1, Principal Investigator: Guy Julier (Leeds Metropolitan University), Co-Investigator: Liz Moor (Middlesex University)

economy has never been more acute. Stepping back from promoting team work and multidisciplinary study, the Design Skills Advisory Panel (2007) sees these as following on from a deeper specialism in specific design disciplines. This may be read from the point of view of a need for specialised skills as being the entry point for design graduates. It may alternatively be seen as a continuation of a certain disciplinary status quo within the tradition of design education.

Beyond Design Disciplines: Social Agency and Commercial Expediency

Through reference to McDowell (1999), Mendoza et al. (2007) view the attempt to define boundaries of design disciplines through dominance and control as a specifically masculine approach. Similarly, Clegg and Mayfield (1999) have argued that notions of the workshop and making reinforce a particular, bounded conception of design that continues to be wrapped up in male domination of the field. Mendoza et al. argue that the energies expended in shoring up a disciplinary approach to design prevent a wider development of creativity.

Equally, Smith (2005) noted that the creation of disciplines within the bureaucratic structures of universities encourages their 'ossification' (Smith, 2005). Upon the development of an academic discipline, so standards and norms of teaching delivery are established and 'canonical' texts are developed that provide a 'tick-box' level of legitimation for study in order to meet targets and provide performance indicators. In its turn, this then restricts the field of study, tying it down to a specific *modus operandi* that ignores the very flexibility and instability of its own object of study. Equally, as design rapidly evolves, reorganising its professional make-up, entering into new contexts of application, innovating relations with its clients and users and being positioned into new ideological structures, so a fixity of analytical and pedagogic approach becomes less and less appropriate.

Challenges to traditional design disciplines have also come from within the industry itself. As the shift towards service economy, or rather a tighter, more orchestrated fit between product and service delivery, has come about in the developed world, so design's relationship to other forms of business, and indeed other academic disciplines, has shifted. Here are some examples on the way that this has impacted on design practices.

In some cases the work of the designer has become 'dematerialised'. David Scothron of Product First states that since most of their clients these days have their own in-house technical product design teams, the work of his small consultancy has moved in recent years toward developing product strategies, concepts and ideas. So they don't do so much product resolution anymore. Instead, they have become product, management, brand and marketing consultants rolled into one (Scothron 2007). TheoryB, a York-based consultancy, engages designers in helping companies develop their creative thinking. This is where they are involved entirely in the 'below the line' aspects of a company – the part that the public doesn't see. Scandal and debate broke out in the pages of *DesignWeek* in 2005 as Hilary Cottam achieved the Design Museum Designer of the Year Award. With a background in anthropology, her work is in managing teams in developing new public sector service deliveries such as in schools and prisons. She admits to not ever having specifically designed anything herself. Her role is in design research, ideation and management.

In other cases, the material outcome of design has become less pre-defined. Heads Together, a Huddersfield-based group, work strategically as catalysts by putting communities at the centre of the decision-making process in the regeneration of their localities. Their role is not in deciding the end-form for improving neighbourhoods, but in facilitating the interface between end-user and a constellation of creative experts. Designers play a role when needed. This may be in helping communities to imagine alternative environments for themselves. It may be resolving the visual or material outcome of those aspirations.

There is also a growing demand for people working as 'brokers' of design. For example, each Primary Care Trust in the National Health Service has a 'design champion' on its Board of Directors whose role is to oversee design quality and the patient environment. Some business schools on both sides of the Atlantic have moved towards integrating design thinking into their programmes. The DSchool at Stanford University and the Said Business School at Oxford University in particular, are generating courses and research foci that use design processes within business strategy developments.

This all suggests a turn towards designers working in more strategic ways where their ideas and innovations play a more significant role in relation to the role of the objects. The 2006 British Design Valuation Survey (Horn, Maxine J. et al. 2006) claims that there is an ever widening gap within the design industry between those consultancies offering more traditional design services – such as designing layouts for brochures or retail interiors – and those that are engaged in more strategic thinking.

Does this mean that design education should similarly be two-tiered – not by a split between vocational and academic approaches but between the technical/aesthetic and the strategic/conceptual?

This Janus-like quandary of design pedagogy is reflected in theory and reality. Sustainability doyen, Ezio Manzini argues that:

> Today design, understood not only as an operative method but also as culture, is oriented in two directions: the one aiming towards isolation, focusing on the formal qualities of products with the most evident aesthetic content (the predominant trend during the 1980s). The other approach consists in facing the present-day challenges, and intervening on the strategies that determine the social and environmental quality of the changing world of today. (Manzini,1998, p.57)

Manzini views the foundation of the more multidisciplinary, strategic designer through the lens of a requirement for social and environmental change setting this against (high) design that is concerned with the fashioning of the object.

By contrast, brand designer Simon Myers sees this duality more as a function of its changing commercial context. In order to offer a viable service, in order to make a living, design expertise must be concentrated in one of two ways. The first is in finding ways of delivering cost-efficient design through, for example, materials sourcing, the optimisation of manufacture and/or assembly processes or building distribution efficiency and balancing these against utilitarian, legal or aesthetic demands. Here, the designer's offer lies in organisational and technical as well as creative prowess. Typically, the concentration is high volume, low cost graphic, spatial or industrial products. The second, alternative model of design consultancy focuses much more on design's strategic role for clients. Its offer lies in the high value, sometimes low volume end of design to deliver bespoke projects and provide personalised insight (Myers, 2007).

Of course, the compelling stimulant to either of these versions of design is its globalisation. With outsourcing of manufacture and, increasingly, parts of the design process itself to the Indian sub-continent and the Far East, designUK's focus has to be increasingly sharp. Equally, the 'democratisation' of technologies – where access to high-specification digital technologies is ever wider – implies ever greater pressure on what it means to be a professional designer.

Design has necessarily adopted a precarious professional identity. Too responsive, driven by the need for differentiation, reinvention and flexibility, designers or design policy makers have rarely dared nail it down to normative curricula, professional body approvals systems and agreed working practices as, for example, architecture has.

There is a quandary here. A drive toward the embedding of design practice in systems thinking and the associated loosening of boundaries between itself and other commercial and civic professional disciplines suggests that, if design education is to be responsive to industry demands, then it should similarly turn itself inside out to concentrate perhaps less on the formal qualities of objects and more on building suites of skills, attitudes and sensibilities that overlap with marketing and business studies but also anthropology, sociology and cultural geography. In advocating more team and multidisciplinary experience in design education, the Design Skills Advisory Panel (2007) goes some way toward encouraging this.

Design Consumption

If we are to believe Featherstone (1991), consumption in the developed world is becoming increasingly aestheticized. Much glib writing (Foster, 2002) has been expended on the growing designerliness of (post)modern culture. But it is more instructive to begin to review different modalities of consumption and the role of design therein.

In recent years it has become more dualistic. Marketing intelligence (PricewaterhouseCooper, 2007) suggests that rational and irrational consumption are being offset against one another. Middlebrow consumption of domestic goods – TVs, furniture, cars – has decreased in value as, thanks mostly to the exploitation of labour in the Far East, these have become cheaper. Alternatively, then, the growth spots for entrepreneurs working in leisure and value-added services have been at the low cost and the luxury ends, hence the growth of EasyJet and TopShop at one end of the market and Gordon Ramsay restaurants and Harvey Nichols at the other. (This doesn't necessarily reflect increasing divisions in society between the poor and the rich. The one in four children and their families who currently live below the poverty line in the UK are well out of the frame.) Instead, middle-range consumers calculate the savings they make on some services, such as flights, and spend these on luxuries.

But what binds the two ends of this spectrum is that the design hardware that focuses their use is hard-wired into systems. EasyJet isn't just a set of aeroplanes or logos. It is a reasonably transparent accounting and service delivery system. Likewise, the fashion-label Prada engages its tightly controlled system of mediation – retail – in order to maintain high design value. The growth of 'lifestyle', 'boutique' or 'design' hotels – the fastest growing sub-sector of a fast growing service sector – is thus to be found in both these camps. The cut-price, but designerly Yotel provides an environment and service for saving money which can later be spent at the more luxurious Malmaison. Each is highly aestheticized, requiring often 'name' designers to boost their cachet. Each exist as part of national or even global networks of service delivery.

This dualism isn't quite the same as the one experienced by Myers, discussed earlier. The low cost products and services are subject to both the production-led and ideas driven design as are the luxury ones. Equally, the dualism described by Manzini impacts on either end of this model of consumption. In other words, issues of environment, social benefit, cost, value and aesthetic experience may be combined in various configurations. What is different, however, is that the design processes involved now go beyond the object and into the systems that both contain it and provide the infrastructures through which it flows.

This is the culture of design in which our students live and in which they also practice. It is one in which both a high level of designer value exists but also in which these values are formatted through various planes. Design, in other words, can go beyond the object to take part in the configuration of systems that mediate flows of information and goods.

How is design to be represented, exhibited, understood, analysed or discussed if it is to be so multi-faceted, played through so many different temporalities, intentions and environments?

Concluding Remarks

I want to conclude by making a set of perhaps provocative proposals about the roles of history, theory and critique in the context of design pedagogy that attempt to address the questions I have raised in my survey of systems, boundaries and valorization in the design profession.

Firstly, how do we deal with the increasing complexity of the design industry? The representation of design urgently needs revision in order to communicate the complexity of its new conditions. For example, if the design history of modernism is to be taught, this should be done in the context of talking about how modernism, and a modernist way of seeing, came to dominate design discourses of the twentieth century and latterly the pages of *Wallpaper** magazine. Equally, the degree show largely continues to exist within this modernist canon, often leading to misapprehensions on the part of external examiners and design journalists alike. It needs tearing up and reactivating in more socially, culturally and economically engaged ways. If the way in which design is represented, in the lecture theatre or in the degree show, is revised, then some chance of building a complex view of design practice stands.

Secondly, should a dualistic approach to design education that respects the separate demands of industry and academia or vocation and scholarship be developed? Or equally, could design pedagogy be divided along Myers's demarcation, that is, between production-led and ideas-driven design? The problem is that the so-called 'demands of industry' are rarely defined. Which industries are being referred to? The design industry? If so, which sector or segment? Form or content-led design? Are these so separate after all? If we are to look at design that services the client end, then which clients are we talking about? Given these challenges to the division, it would seem appropriate to vigorously resist attempts to pin design education down into procedures and norms that are pushed in one direction or the other.

Thirdly, how can the professional shifts towards complexity and interdisciplinarity and the demand for individuality be mediated within design pedagogy? How can teamwork and egos be balanced? I think the answer lies in the notion that part of scholarly development is about developing an individual, focused and defendable point of view on something. This is as true for subjects in the sciences, humanities and the social sciences as it is in design. It's just that it's done in more visible and spectacular ways in design. So, currently, *contra* Angela McRobbie, I'm comfortable with the notion of students fashioning themselves if that demands of them that they rigorously define what their position is. I *want* them to be both reflective and reflexive practitioners. And that in turn means that they understand the worthwhile contributions they can make in terms of the creation of value. This might be commercial value, but may also be social, cultural, environmental, political and symbolic values.

Design culture is a term that has emerged within the profession and academia for the last five years or so. It is variously used to denote collectively, locationally and temporally understood processes and attitudes, infrastructures and values. It also assumes, for some, to be something that can be encultured, fashioned or ameliorated (Julier, 2006). It is something that can be observed and enacted upon; it is a pre-existing set of circumstances but also an activity or process. Practising design culture involves both action in and reflection on the complex arrangements and relationships that characterise this era of advanced, disorganised capitalism. In these conditions, the need for 'knowing' practitioners is ever more pressing.

Bibliography

Clegg, S. & Mayfield, W. (1999) 'Gendered by Design: How Women's Place in Design is Still Defined by Gender' *Design Issues*, Vol. 15, No. 3 pp.3–16

Design Skills Advisory Panel (2007) 'High Level Skills for Higher Value' (report) London, Design Council and Creative & Cultural Skills

Foster, H. (2002) *Design and Crime (And Other Diatribes)* London, Verso

Frith, S. & Horne, H. (1987) *Art into Pop* London, Routledge

Hollington, G. (1998) 'The Usual Suspects' *Design*, Summer, pp.62–3

Horn, M. J. (et al.) (2006) 'The British Design Industry Valuation Survey, 2005 to 2006', (report) Brighton, British Design Innovation

Julier, G. (2006) 'From Visual Culture to Design Culture' *Design Issues* Vol. 22, No. 1 pp.64–76

Manzini, Ezio (1998) 'Products in a Period of Transition: Products, Services and Interactions for a Sustainable Society', in Tevfik Balcioglu (Ed.) *The Role of Product Design in Post-Industrial Society* Ankara, Middle East Technical University pp.43–58

McDowell, L. (1999) *Gender, Identity and Place: Understanding Feminist Geographies* Minneapolis, University of Minnesota Press

McRobbie, A. (2007) 'The Los Angelisation of London Three short-waves of young people's micro-economies of culture and creativity in the UK' in *Transversal* available at <http://eipcp.net/transversal/0207/mcrobbie/en> 09/01/2008

Mendoza, H. R., Bernasconi C.& MacDonald, N.M(2007) 'Creating New Identities in Design Education' in *Journal of Art and Design Education* Vol. 26 No. 3 pp.308–13

Myers, S. (2007) 'Just have the balls to say 'no', in *Design Week* 04/10/07

PricewaterhouseCoopers (2007) 'Lifestyle Hotels Survey' (report) London, PricewaterhouseCoopers

Scothron, D. (2007) Product designer, Product First. Intervention at 'Counting Creativity: the Organisation and Valorisation of Design Practices', workshop, Design Council, London, Wednesday 17 January, 2007

Smith, M. (2005) 'Visual Studies, or the ossification of thought' *Journal of Visual Culture*, Vol. 4, No. 2 pp.237–56

Chapter 2

Let's all go shoplifting:
Culture, Consumerism and Education[1]

Gen Doy
De Montfort University

Before I arrive at the material relating to the title of this paper, I want to briefly set out some preliminary contextual remarks and describe my own positioning as an educator. I am not a designer, nor even a design historian, and my approach to the teaching of designers is one closely informed by the study of visual culture and cultural studies. I have, in the last few years, been teaching critical and cultural theories to MA design students from a wide range of disciplines. This came about partly because our undergraduate and postgraduate art and design history degrees at De Montfort University, Leicester, were closed down, and partly because I am interested in theory, debates and ideas, and our Faculty of Art and Design decided, rightly in my view, that design students would benefit from encounters with theories and methods from disciplines other than design. Some of the thinking behind this relates to the Faculty of Art and Design's response to the Research Assessment Exercise (RAE), a highly bureaucratic exercise which takes place every five years or so to determine the allocation of research funding in British universities. (For a more detailed and political critique of the RAE see Callinicos, 2006.) In the course of preparation for the RAE, it emerged that some designers and other practitioners were not accustomed to writing in a theoretical, scholarly way about their work or presenting it as research. Thus, interdisciplinarity emerged as an essential element in design research, since many theories were located elsewhere and then they 'migrated' across the borders of disciplines into design practice, finding a home there and 'belonging', to a greater or lesser extent. These theoretical 'incomers' from other disciplines would, supposedly, enliven and improve the existing design culture. Some welcomed these migrants, some were resistant to an encounter with them. Already notions of migration, displacement and belonging are emerging here. Now, whether you agree or disagree with what has taken place in my university, and in others, you can see that in the smaller specialist domains of design, cultural theory and academic teaching and research, there are parallels with much bigger issues concerning economics, politics, geography and capitalism. Clearly this is no accident. In fact many of the things I want to look at in this talk are also related to wider topics, such as consumerism, ownership and empowerment, which all exist in what has become the global marketplace of higher education. I should point out here that many of the MA design students to whom I teach cultural

---

1. I want to thank Kate Hatton for her invitation to address the Design and Pedagogy conference, and for discussing with me preliminary ideas for my talk which gave rise to this essay.

theory, speak and write English as a second language, and often come from teaching traditions which are very different from the situation they encounter with me in Leicester. I want them to think for themselves, develop their own ideas, and speak in the first person using 'I', some of which they have not been encouraged to do previously. Many of the MA students, including some of the 'home' students, are expecting a continuation of their undergraduate experiences where they have sometimes been encouraged to accumulate knowledge in the form of facts, information, and sources for their own designs, rather than critical, analytical tools, and to develop technical skills rather than question the purpose of these skills and their apparent neutrality.

At a higher level, that of M.Phil./Ph.D. students, I was awarded grants from the Arts and Humanities Research Council (AHRC) in collaboration with Dr. Jane Tormey of The Loughborough University School of Art and Design. We encouraged and guided our postgraduate students to organise a successful conference on the theme of 'In Theory? Encounters with Theory in practice-based Art and Design Research' (June 2007) and now have an AHRC grant for academic years 2008–9 to organise workshops and a two-day student-run conference on 'Creative Interdisciplinarity in Art and Design Research'. These initiatives are designed to facilitate creative thinking across traditional academic disciplines, encourage students to be adventurous in bringing together theories and practices, and, above all, to help them enjoy their research activities.

If I were a designer, I imagine I would probably look first at examples of practice and the processes of invention and making to provide me with these critical and analytical tools, but as I am a writer, reader, and a looker, I turn to texts and visual material to help me think and move forward. So, this is the 'background', if you want to call it that, to what follows.

After discussion with Kate Hatton, I decided for my conference talk and this subsequent essay to think about, and follow through, some analogies and metaphors of shopping and shoplifting in relation to theory, research and design education. Shortly after the conference, I thought more about the commodification of education in the process of reading the book by Lewis Hyde, *The Gift* (Hyde, 2006). My presentation of these thoughts here is based on quite fluid and general comparisons and analogies, and is not intended to be rigid or prescriptive.

I first thought about shoplifting years ago when I was at school, but did not do a lot of it, partly through fear of being caught, and partly because I had no need to steal the kinds of things that I wanted, such as books, because my parents were keen to buy them for me. Then a few years ago I thought about shoplifting again. Researching a book about drapery and its meanings in visual culture, from Renaissance drawings to shop window displays and newspaper images (Doy, 2002), I came across photographs of North African men and women wearing draped clothing, taken in the second decade of the twentieth century by Gaëtan de Clérambault, a Parisian police psychiatrist. I read books about de Clérambault, books written by him, and studied the archive of his photographs and writings in Paris in the library of the former Musée de l'Homme.[2] One of his texts was devoted to his 'analysis' – interrogation would be a more precise term – of women arrested for stealing fabric, especially heavy silk, in Parisian department stores, which they then used as an aid to masturbation. De Clérambault's articles based on his findings were originally published in 1908 and 1910 in the *Revue des Archives d'Anthropologie Criminelle*, and reissued as *Passion Erotique des Etoffes chez la Femme*, in 1997 (de Clérambault, 1997). As I read further, I discovered that this was not just something related to the poorer women who ended up in prison and as the subjects (objects would be more accurate) of de Clérambault's articles, but it was an issue that affected many women from all classes of society.

---

2. For the best published selection of de Clerambault's fascinating photographs see Tisseron, ed., 1990.

(Interestingly, there seems to be little on male shoplifters at this time as compared to female ones). As the big department stores developed in the mid-late nineteenth-century, tantalising and seductive displays of goods laid out under new forms of artificial lighting worked only too well ... not only were people lured into the stores to buy, they were also unable to resist the urge to steal. Emile Zola's famous novel, *Au Bonheur des Dames*, (*The Ladies' Paradise*) published in 1882, situates a relationship between a young shopgirl and a department store owner in the heady atmosphere of a profusion of fetished commodities displayed in the shop which gives its name to the novel (Zola, 1882). The customers are tempted, sensually excited, and eventually seduced by the merchandise on show. Zola describes such an alluring display of fabrics thus:

> Starting from the dull shades of the calico and linen, and the heavy shades of the flannel and cloth, there then came the velvet, silk and satin goods – quite an ascending gamut, the white gradually lighted up, finishing in little flames at the breaks of the folds ... all this cambric and muslin, dead, scattered over the counters, thrown about, heaped up, was going to become living, with the life of the flesh, odorous and warm with the odour of love, a white cloud become sacred, bathed in light, and of which the least flutter, the pink of a knee disclosed through the whiteness, ravaged the world. (Zola, 1882, pp.353–4)

Now, how does this scene described in the novel relate to academic research and teaching? In a way, when a practice-based student encounters theory, displayed like the textiles in the department store, I hope that their practice is going to make it come alive – a sensous practice endowed with consciousness. A student, nowadays often termed a client or a customer or a stakeholder, depending on which university or government document you read, is a bit like the department store customer, except that now s/he has to pay before even getting through the door to the consumption stage. Before the students' eyes and intellects, all the theories, debates, and controversies are assembled and available either in paper form, electronically or through the lecturers' words, both spoken and written. Students now arrive like shoppers, already positioned within a pre-organised capitalist system based on the exchange of money for services and products, and eventually, a degree within the knowledge economy.

As I was writing this, though, I wondered whether this analogy with the nineteenth-century department store was appropriate. The way in which the intellectual commodities are displayed to the students is not nearly as sensually enticing as the goods in a shop or window display. Slides, visual materials and actual objects can certainly enliven classes, but are obviously not as seductive, and perhaps we ought to think more about this comparison between the sensual attractions of consumerism and the ways in which the, hopefully, more significant attractions of creative and intellectual life are presented. But is the answer – to try to make our classes compete with the lure and excitement generated by shopping? I think that where we really can make a difference is by seducing the mind, rather than mainly appealing to the senses. My apologies for the tendency to suggest a Cartesian mind/body split here, and perhaps it would be more accurate to advocate appeals to the mind with and through the senses. The experience of shopping, pleasurable though it is, can never, for me, be as satisfying as finding something new for my brain to enjoy, and I think that is what I would like my students to feel as well. And I hope that I can persuade students to share this view through encountering, and developing for themselves, critical and cultural theories and debates, whether they are design students or students of other disciplines.

However, to return to the notion of the consumer ... A number of academics from cultural studies backgrounds who write on consumerism and the self have argued that consumption requires particular skills, which are developed and honed by individuals in a process of constructing their self-identities and subjectivities. For example, Angela Partington, in her essay on perfume and packaging written in the 1990s, which my students continue to find really enjoyable, argued that consumption should not be criticised by, for example, feminists, as it is an example of skilled and inventive agency:

> Consumption is for most of us the only place where desires can be expressed and freedoms exercised, and therefore it is a source of power. (Partington, 1996, p.205)

While many academic disciplines have been influenced by postmodern theories in their critique of the so-called Cartesian, modernist and autonomous subject, preferring views of the self which see it as fragmented and 'in process of construction', Roy Boyne has pointed out that there is an important exception. Economics is different, he writes, since the ideology of capitalist economics requires that the decision to work or to buy is a result of rational choice and agency, and therefore requires subjectivity (Boyne, 1991, p.45). Although some scholars are critical of the positive emphasis on consumerism as a site of agency and even of freedom, the previously mentioned authors, as well as Daniel Miller, for example, see shopping as not so much negative but as empowering, 'the act of a home-making (as distinct from a homeless) mind', and consumption therefore becomes productive, cultural 'work' (Agnew, 1993, p.30). Miller's espousal of shopping as self-fashioning and self-affirmative (for example in Miller, 1998) is very different from the position of Conrad Lodziak, who argues that we are forced to consume because, with the hegemony of capitalism and the generalisation of alienated labour, we can no longer produce to satisfy our own needs and have to buy products which were previously made in the home or the locality (Lodziak, 2002).

Now, it occurred to me as I was reading material about shops and shoplifters, that the arguments which Partington and others put forward about shopping, the self, and agency, could be applied just as well to shoplifting. Indeed, it could be argued that the shoplifter is even more skilled and resourceful than the shopper. If we accept the argument that the self is empowered and playfully constructed through the 'legitimate' purchasing of goods which enhance the subject's sense of self and identity, then what is wrong with applying the same arguments to theft? The positive glosses on consumerism certainly appear to ignore the situation of the destitute and the homeless, who, presumably, are not able to construct a self for themselves by shopping, since they do not have disposable income. So while I was researching my book, *Picturing the Self*, I looked at the literature on shoplifting, including sources I found on the Internet as well as libraries (Doy, 2005, pp.167–70).

Class, 'race', age and celebrity influence the likelihood of prosecution for shoplifters. Black people are more likely to be charged when arrested for shoplifting, as are homeless people (Klemke, 1992, p51, p.63). The actress Winona Ryder escaped lightly after being convicted of shoplifting in 2002 (her defence was that she was researching a role for a film), whereas a poor Californian man, Leonardo Andrade, was jailed for fifty years under the 'three strikes' ruling, for stealing one hundred and fifty-four dollars-worth of videos for his family to watch (Campbell, 2002, pp.2–3). Klemke, interestingly, suggests that shoplifting can also allow alienated individuals to express their creativity and individuality (Klemke, 1992, pp.78–9, p.92).

There is a thought-provoking passage in *Theories of Surplus Value*, where Marx argues that even crime under capitalism is productive; the development of judicial treatises, security devices, the building of prisons, work for lawyers and the police, and jobs for lecturers in law departments are all examples (Marx, 1979, pp.167–8). Another document on the creativity of crime under capitalism, though less famous than that of Karl Marx, was a website I found entitled 'Why I love shoplifting from big corporations'. The author of the article on this website encourages shoplifting as a form of 'refusal of the exchange economy', a statement against the alienation of the modern 'consumer' and a 'moral activity' in the case of theft from unethical big corporations, such as those which damage the environment. The final paragraph reads:

> Shoplifting divests commodities (and the marketplace in general) of the mythical power they seem to have to control the lives of consumers ... when they are seized by force, they show themselves for what they are: merely resources that have been held by force by these corporations at the expense of everyone else. Shoplifting places us back in the physical world, where things are real, where things are nothing more than their physical characteristics (weight, taste, ease of acquisition) and are not invested with superstitious qualities such as 'market value' and 'profit margin' ... Perhaps shoplifting alone will not be able to overthrow industrial society or the capitalist system ... but in the meantime it is one of the best forms of protest and self empowerment. (Anon., 2002, p.1)

The same spirited denial of big business commodification of existence is evident in the short film with a neo-punk soundtrack, *Why I love shoplifting from big Corporations* (2005) by Franklin Lopez. Inspired by a chapter from the book *Days of War, Nights of Love*, by crimethinc (from which the above quote is taken) this can be viewed on the website www.archive.org/details/shoplifting (accessed 17.3.2008).

What can we learn then, from these analogies between shopping, shoplifting and design education (or any other education for that matter)? Universities are being increasingly privatised, their services commodified, and the students positioned as consumers who can buy what universities have to offer. Are the choices open to them restricted to (1) shopping as a well-behaved consumer supposedly constructing various postmodern identities, or (2) shoplifting as either a thief or a radical subversive? Bill Readings, in his stimulating book *The University in Ruins*, 1996, argues that universities are no longer interested in culture, but in a 'techo-bureaucratic notion of excellence'. He maintains that 'what gets taught or researched matters less than the fact that it be excellently taught or researched' (Readings, 1996, pp.13–14). He states that culture no longer matters to the managers of advanced capitalism, and that they promote and advertise their 'striving for excellence' ... in knowledge transfer, income generation, teaching and even in one instance in car parking (for example Readings, 1996, p.105). Universities increasingly promote themselves in similar ways to businesses, and indeed nation-states in which universities function are managed like huge corporations.

What does this situation mean for the educator and the student? Viewed at its most dismal, the educator is like the salesperson in the department store of the university. On a really basic level we lecturers can give the students some pre-digested material, lecture summaries and so on, to enable them to 'pass' with little effort, or we can lay out before them seductively displayed theories by Marx (ironically), Freud, Lacan, Bourdieu, Baudrillard, etc. But how to tempt the students to 'buy' into them (a suggestive expression), or to take them home on sale or return? I don't want to push this analogy too far and distort the points I want us to consider, but it is important to me to avoid making my students into consumers, despite the fact that many of them want to go out and start their own businesses and cater for a consumerist clientele. This is mostly unavoidable. So how do we tempt students into trying without buying (into the system)? Maybe the shoplifting analogy has something to offer.

With shoplifting, the thief has accomplished something without the knowledge of the shop and its personnel, and feels that s/he 'has got away with something'. The shoplifter has stepped outside the rules of the system, which is not always a bad thing for students and academics to do. Yet clearly breaking rules in and of itself is not particularly progressive, for example in the case of plagiarism, which is theft of a different kind. Our political and social views influence what forms of behaviour we may support in our students. Also, once shoplifters have the item, they may not use it themselves but sell it on. The item and its meaning do not influence their thinking, though the process of acquiring it perhaps did.[3]

Shopping and shoplifting also relate to where you get the theories and ideas from. The shopper is restricted by financial constraints and may only buy one or two things, textbooks perhaps, and will stick with them even if they are not quite providing the intellectual stimulation and excitement of encountering something genuinely new and useful which shifts her/his mind into a higher gear. The shoplifter, on the other hand, is more able to visit different disciplines, and a variety of sources, because s/he has not invested heavily in a small number of items. I'm not only talking literally of students buying books here (which doesn't seem to happen as often as it should, for various reasons) but of mental attitudes. However there is often a bewildering range of material on display and students can be confused and intimidated by this, rather than stimulated. Also, some students are comfortable within the boundaries of their chosen discipline, and have no wish to either shop or shoplift in other locations. For this type of student, interdisciplinarity and the engagement with ideas from other subject areas is seen as a distraction and takes up time that could be used for practical design work.

Student comments on the MA/MSc. module I organise, *Design in Contexts*, range from the totally negative ('It was not relevant to my work') to the enthusiastic ('I thought *Design in Contexts* was really useful and made you consider the wider implications of your designs; this is something you do not do at BA level. In the ecological and political climate it raises many relevant moral questions which go beyond the goals of aesthetics and functions of the designed object'.)

The students have one piece of written work to complete on this module (the other assessment is a group presentation on a selected text: book, book chapter, article etc. which engages with theories and methods). The written piece is a workbook in three sections of about four thousand words. The outline of the brief is as follows.

1. An introduction motivating the selection of at least one and not more than three written texts dealing with theories and issues in design criticism and analysis.

2. The analysis and application of key aspects of these written texts to the work of a selected designer or designers.

3. The relevance of the selected writings, theories and issues to the student's own design practice and research.

Students who want to creatively interpret this brief can do so as long as they check first with the tutor. For example, there was a workbook written in the style of Derrida's book *Glas*, with a creative graphic layout and text (Derrida, 1990). Another student used ideas from Barthes, Judith Williamson and an article on colour as semiotic mode by Guenther Kress to analyse work by a Brazilian graphic designer Adhemas Batista, and then discuss all this in relation to her own current work and future plans. There was also a lovely piece of work where the student selected a text by David Dabydeen on 'Teaching West

---

3. After my talk, another academic at the conference suggested to me that it might be worth thinking about the idea of smuggling as another alternative to consumerism in education. This might be worth pursuing, though I have not had the opportunity to develop this yet.

Indian Literature in Britain', and used ideas from this to discuss objects, their creation and their history (Dabydeen, 2003). The objects were allowed to speak about their past and their presence in a moving way, making reference to slavery and 'racial' oppression. A glass chair by designer Danny Lane, (1988, Victoria and Albert Museum) is one of the design objects discussed. The chair is made up of hundreds of separate drilled pieces of toughened glass held together by a central steel bolt. The edges look rough, and the chair uncomfortable. In his workbook, the student asks the chair a number of questions, including:

> Who can sit upon this throne in comfort? Would it be sweet like cane sugar or soft like the cotton on your back? It may turn out to be as hot as neat rum direct from the bottle ... Every element each boy and girl, brother, sister, mother and father have been pressed one upon another held by steel flesh to flesh. Each extended across silicone sands to be held frozen in toil.
>
> Bodies crack to hold this map aloft for so long, so you may rest your bones awhile.

The chair speaks back:

> ... Each segment is faceted, a cultural mixture, not bolted to any one idea. I stand-alone in the room, I should be seen as complete and whole. I have been reassembled from the shattered remains of rejected misfits; so I am a symbol of rebirth.
>
> Note how my fragments refract the white light recreating a prism of colour on your face; I cast a post-modernist rainbow to confound your stereotypes. (Ross, 2006, p.11, quoted with the student's permission)[4]

Some time after this student had completed the workbook, I gave him a photocopy of Janet Hoskins' essay 'Agency, Biography and Objects' which had just been published in Chris Tilley et al. eds., *Handbook of Material Culture* (Hoskins, 2006). It was encouraging for this student to discover that what he had already done in his assignment, using his own creative interpretation of texts about Black writing, turned out to be an example of the approach theorised and later published by Hoskins. However, these examples of student workbooks, and the poetic and creative approach of Ross in particular, seem to me to go beyond the possibilities of both the shopping and the shoplifting strategies for teachers and students alike. Similarly, I was touched by a recent message from another MA student, from India but now teaching in Shanghai, who, in one seminar discussion had become frustrated and declared, 'What do I need to discuss gender and stuff for? I just want to be a designer'. His message told me how much he was enjoying his new lecturing post, the enthusiasm of his students, and how much he had learned from me as a teacher and a helper. He had asked me for advice on teaching before he left, and I told him that he would not go wrong if he supported the students, talked with them to discover what they wanted to do, and then helped them to do it. These fruitful relationships in education are no longer those of shopping or shoplifting, but of giving and mutual enrichment.

I recently read carefully through the book by Lewis Hyde, *The Gift* (Hyde, 2006). While I found it a thought-provoking and sensitive book, there were some aspects of Hyde's approach that I disagreed with, for example his view that the artistic gift (the gift of artistic creativity) is a mystery: 'We cannot know these things by way of economic, psychological, or aesthetic theories' (Hyde, 2006, p.283). Also, Hyde appears to believe that highly artistic and creative people ('gifted' people) have this almost

---

4. Grateful thanks to Michael Ross and Katrin Suess for allowing me to mention their work here.

fabulous endowment which cannot be taught. As a teacher and researcher, I think that while obviously some people are truly outstanding and talented, everyone can develop in ways which they probably did not envisage when they started out on their degree or in other forms of education. However, these criticisms aside, Hyde's main arguments are very interesting in terms of thinking about art and design education, or indeed any education. Hyde begins by looking at folktales and customs of gift-giving in 'tribal' and small-group societies, and compares these to the ways in which the work of creative art is like a gift. When it becomes completely commodified, it is destroyed as art. The gift should not be capitalised upon, but passed on, or returned in some form, enhancing the life-experience of each giver, who is therefore always a giver and recipient. The gift of creative art becomes more abundant as it is given away. Hyde relates this to erotic life and love, pointing out that libido is not lost when it is given away (Hyde, p.26). He adds that 'in gift exchange it, the increase, stays in motion and follows the object, while in commodity exchange it stays behind as profit' (Hyde, p.39). Teaching under capitalism is placed in a difficult position, and so are jobs like nursing. Basically, teaching is based on giving, but the labour of the teacher is commodified as the teacher sells her/his labour to live. Also teachers cannot continually 'give', over and above reasonable weekly working hours without eventually damaging their own quality of life. Hyde comments that obviously few jobs are 'pure gift labors',

> but any portion of gift labor in a job will tend to pull it out of the market and make it a less lucrative – and a 'female' – profession ... In a modern, capitalist nation, to labour with gifts (and to treat them as gifts, rather than exploit them) remains a mark of the female gender (Hyde, 2006, pp.109–110).

In his 'Afterword', written in 2006 though, Hyde feels that the boundary between gifts and commodities is permeable, and less rigid than he thought when he originally wrote his book in the late 1970s. When I looked at my relationships with the students and their work, I felt that there was much in Hyde's book which could be applied to our situation. I am paid to work in a university; the students, especially the economically-penalised overseas ones who are charged elevated fees, pay to 'consume' the course. However, when teaching and student development are at their best, a gift relationship supersedes consumerism, commodification, and profit-making in Higher Education. I give to the students aspects of myself, my thoughts, my experience, and they give it back enhanced to me or to other students. The gift moves on, nourished and enhanced, and does not remain behind as profit.

In conclusion, returning to the analogy of shopping and shoplifting, I would say that neither is quite the approach I want to encourage in the students, but if pushed, I would say I would rather have shoplifters than shoppers. Ideally, what I want to encourage by guiding students towards the integration of theories and practices through interdisciplinary research, is the emergence of an empowered and conscious person who can articulate analysis and criticism embodied in creative practice as well as in writing. The result of this, hopefully, will be creative people who can voice informed criticisms of the systems they work within with a view to changing them, rather than the underhand and secret sabotage of the shoplifter, or the ludic self-centered consumerism of the shopper. Even the notion of the gift, while probably more fruitful than the other strategies, nonetheless only partially subverts the existing institutional structures of higher education. Hopefully it gives us a pointer to ways in which teaching and creativity can be so much more enriching in contexts which, one day I hope, will not be capitalist.

Bibliography

Agnew, J.C. (1993) 'Coming up for air. Consumer Culture in Historical Perspective' in Brewer, J. and Porter, R. (Eds) *Consumption and the World of Goods* London and New York, Routledge pp.19–39

Anon. (2002) 'Why I love shoplifting from big corporations', <http://www.crimethinc.com/library/shoplifting.html> (24/08/2002)

Boyne, R. (1991) *Subject, Society and Culture* London, Sage

de Clérambault, G.G. (1997) *Passion Erotique des Etoffes chez la Femme* Le Plessis-Robinson, Synthélabo

Callinicos, A. (2006) *Universities in a neoliberal World* London, Bookmarks

Campbell, D.(2002) 'Show Trial', *Guardian Review* November 8, pp.2–3

Dabydeen, D.(2003) 'Teaching West Indian Literature in Britain' in Bassnett S.(Ed.) *Studying British Cultures An Introduction* revised edition, London/New York, Routledge, pp.139–55

Derrida, J. (1990) *Glas* Lincoln, Nebraska, University of Nebraska Press

Doy, G. (2002) *Drapery: Classicism and Barbarism in Visual Culture* London and New York, I.B.Tauris

Doy, G. (2005) *Picturing the Self. Changing Views of the Subject in Visual Culture* London/New York, I.B.Tauris

Hyde, L. (1979, 2006) *The Gift. How the Creative Spirit Transforms the World* Edinburgh, New York and Melbourne, Canongate

Klemke, L.W. (1992) *The Sociology of Shoplifting: Boosters and Snitches Today* Westport Connecticut and London, Prager

Lodziak, C. (2002) *The Myth of Consumerism* London, Pluto Press

Marx, K. (1979) *Selected Writings in Sociology and Social Philosophy* Bottomore T.B. and Rubel, M. (Eds) Harmondsworth, Penguin

Miller, D. (1998) *A Theory of Shopping* Cambridge, Polity Press

Partington, A.(1996) 'Pleasure, Packaging and Postmodernity', in Kirkham, P. (Ed) *The Gendered Object*, Manchester, Manchester University Press, pp.204–18

Readings, B. (1996) *The University in Ruins* Cambridge Mass., Harvard University Press

Ross, M. O. (2006) *Workbook. Design in Contexts* M.A. Design Innovation, De Montfort University (unpublished)

Tilley, C. (et al.) (Eds.) (2006) *Handbook of Material Culture* London, Thousand Oaks, New Delhi, Sage

Tisseron, S. (Ed.) (1990) *Gaëtan Gatian de Clérambault.Psychiatre et Photographe* Paris, Les Empêcheurs de Penser en Rond

Zola, E. (1882) *The Ladies Paradise* ed. K.Ross, Berkeley L.A./Oxford, University of California Press

18

Chapter 3

Praxeological Subjectification:
The Hidden Power of Practical Activities

Peter Oakley
Bournemouth University/SWLLN

Introduction

In design education the acquisition of practical manipulative skills are usually considered as necessary stages in the development of creative and personal intellectual responses. In contrast, anthropological theory, in particular approaches to production derived from material culture theories, credits objects and their associated manual techniques with the agency to influence practitioners. Jean-Pierre Warnier (2001), starting from this position, and relating it to Schilder's concept of the perceived body image, Foucault's theory of 'subjectification', and Tisseron's psychological theory of 'symbolisation', has constructed a theory of 'praxeological' 'subjectification'. After providing an exposition of the theoretical underpinning of this central conceptual term, the following paper explores how observations from design education can be used to provide evidence that this process is occurring in design practice and considers both the positive and negative implications that its prior existence, or its development, may have on design students. Lastly it proposes productive avenues for further research relating to the subject.

Defining Praxeological Subjectification

The theory of praxeological subjectification is related to the recent burgeoning body of anthropological research concerning material culture, which can arguably be traced back to Appadurai's seminal book *The Social Life of Things* (1986). This interest, however, can best be described as resurgent rather than novel as many of the individuals commonly referred to as the founding fathers[1] of anthropology considered the relationships between subjects and objects of central importance to their field observations. Marcel Mauss, whose famous essay 'The Gift' (2002), demonstrated the crucial role objects can play in social relations, also continually returned to questions thrown up by the interaction

---

1. Two of the most prominent are Bronislaw Malinowski, who focussed on the importance of Kula valuables in the lives of Trobriand Islanders, and Franz Boas, whose work on the Northwest Coast included the importance of the objects used or destroyed during the potlatch ceremonies: coppers, masks, and foodstuffs. Though Marcel Mauss is included in this canon, his contribution was theoretical, drawing on the fieldwork of others and combining them with examples from historical European cultures (Davies 2005; Eriksen 2004).

between subjects and objects in their own right (Schlanger 1998). In his essay 'Techniques of the Body' (2006) first published as '*Les Techniques du Corps*' in 1935, Mauss attempted to conduct a study of 'the ways in which from society to society men know how to use their bodies' (Mauss, 2006: p.78). Despite a declaration that he was going to specifically exclude 'instrumental techniques', the essay returns again and again to interactions between human bodies and objects: diving boards, bugles, drums, shoes, wooden floats, hand axes, hammocks, poles and, in a recollection of his experience of serving with English troops during the First World War, spades:

> The English troops I was with did not know how to use French spades, which forced us to change 8,000 spades a division when we relieved a French division, and vice versa. (Mauss, 2006, p.79)

Mauss recognised that the events he witnessed were more than just a logistical issue, but an exemplar of how culturally specific such apparently commonplace physical activities were. But he was unable to deduce exactly how his subjects assimilated observed physical skills, such as the Kabyle man who was able to walk downstairs in Turkish slippers: 'How can he keep his feet without the slippers coming off? I have tried to see, to do it, but I can't understand' (Mauss, 2006 p.88). It was Mauss's attempt to *see* a solution that was holding him back. The descending Kabyle slipper-wearer was, in fact, *feeling* how he should walk downstairs.

The answer to Mauss's question lay in medical science, and relevant breakthroughs were being made during the same period. In his essay 'The Image and Appearance of the Human Body' (Schilder, 1935) Paul Schilder proposed that any individual's perceived body is not necessarily equivalent to their anatomical structure. That the body even directly perceived itself at all had only been recognised by C.S. Sherrington in the 1890s. Sherrington called this newly discovered sense proprioception, and its fundamental importance to motor skills and a sense of self, as well as the distressing results of its loss, have since become increasingly understood and better documented. Oliver Sacks's descriptions of his neurological patients (Sacks, 1986), describe how partial or complete loss of proprioception leads to a lack of control over the body; everyday tasks such as gripping cutlery or walking require complete focus and observation by the subject in order for the activity to be completed without mishap. The loss of physical control is accompanied by a loss of corporeal self-recognition, as described by 'the man who fell out of bed':

> A man should know his own body, what's his and what's not – but this leg, this thing, doesn't feel right, doesn't feel real, and it doesn't look a part of me. (Sacks, 1986, p.54)

Not only could Sacks's patient not feel that his left leg existed, but the existence of a 'counterfeit' leg that had somehow become attached to him induced shock and terror.

Schilder recognised that as well as contracting, the same perceived body image could extend beyond the anatomical body. Through an *apprenticeship* of repeated action and familiarity, individuals perceptually synthesise with particular instruments; during subsequent use they become a temporarily amalgamated subject-&-object. The blind man, through practice, can feel through the tip of his cane; the woman practised in walking in high heels knows when the point of each of her stilettos has just touched the ground.

Both of these actions are types of *psychometricity*, a term coined by praxeology, the science of motricity. Psychometricity describes the learnt actions of a single individual acting alone; widely experienced examples would be pedalling a bicycle or learning how to grip a pencil in order to write or draw. When physically interacting with others, individuals are engaging in *sociometry*, as in relay racing, where a coordination of movement is necessary to pass the baton whilst running; success often relies on *motor communication* (indication of intended movement and its reading by others) to be carried out effectively. In team sports the movement of other team members can be read because the procedures, whilst varying in response to particular circumstances, follow a recognisable pattern. Such procedures are called *motor algorithms* and their variability separates them from *motor stereotypes,* actions that are utterly repetitive (Warnier, 2001).

One particular set of motor stereotypes, army parade drill, has an important place in the work of Michel Foucault. In his book *Discipline and Punish* (1979) Foucault proposed that the development of army training was one of the factors that fed into the development of *discipline* in the modern age. Disciplinary projects 'called for multiple separations, individualising distributions, an organisation in depth of surveillance and control, an intensification and a ramification of power' (Foucault 1979, p.198). This inequality in social interaction was materialised through structures such as Jeremy Bentham's Panopticon, which was designed to create an environment where incarcerated subjects were separated and potentially continually under scrutiny. The result was self-regulation, an eventual *subjectification* by the observed individual to what they believed the observer's expectations to be. Foucault saw the Panopticon as a physical exemplar of subjectification, but not its apogee. He contended that the disciplinary project has since extended out from its originally marginal position in the prison, army, school and hospital to create an encompassing network throughout the cultural fabric of Western society, an interlocking system of *governmentalities* that subjugate whole populations. This hypothesis was extended in Foucault's later work, *The History of Sexuality*, in particular the introductory volume (Foucault, 1978) where he contends that modern sexuality relates to specific governmentalities rather than being a neutral biological reality.

Though Foucault did identify that 'the forces that drive our history do not so much operate on our thoughts, our social institutions, or even our environment as on our individual bodies' (Gutting, 2005, p.47) he did not hypothesise on how they did so, expecting the reader to accept that this process as obvious and inevitable. This theoretical gap can, however, be bridged by Serge Tisseron's concept of *symbolisation*; 'the process by which a subject introduces into his psychic envelope his experiences of the outside world' (Warnier, 2001, p.14). Internalisation occurs when emotional experience is transformed through one of the three modes of symbolisation: image, language and sensori-motricity. Of the three, sensori-motricity is the most effective in reaching the subject 'in their depths' as it draws on first-hand experience and relates most closely to the emotions and psychic drives. In contrast, the other two modes have to rely on a prior personal sensorimotor experience to trigger understanding of what is to be conveyed. Whilst many of our experiences with objects or other subjects are relatively neutral, in emotional contexts such experiences lead to sensori-affectivo-motor symbolisation as an experience sinks in to the subject's psyche.

In the conclusion to his paper describing praxeological subjectification, Warnier asks 'What is at stake?' (Warnier, 2001, pp.20–22). To indicate an answer he considers the situation of the child soldier, whose long apprenticeship in handling and using firearms in extreme emotional situations results in a very particular and problematic subject-and-object, the child-and-kalachnikov:

A subject cannot be produced and undone like a Lego toy. Once the child-soldier is withdrawn from the armed faction by Unicef or a Non-Governmental Organization, his sensori-affectivo-motor, psychic and discursive retraining is highly problematic, especially in view of the fact that the materialities provided for him offer nothing to be compared with the stock of violent sensations and emotions experienced by him when he/she was armed. Speech alone will not suffice to do the trick (Warnier, 2001, p.21).

Once a child has incorporated a kalachnikov into their perceived self-image it may be possible to physically remove them from a theatre of conflict, but how should the interjected sensori-affectivo-motricity that has become part of their psychological make-up be tackled?

Whilst the situation of the design practitioner or student may not appear to match such extreme circumstances, I would propose that these subjects have also been reached 'in their depths'. It is axiomatic in current UK Art and Design educational practice that new students should undertake technical training to introduce them to the range of core manual processes relevant to their specialism. This is followed by a personal learning programme considered necessary for students to master chosen specific processes at a more advanced level (QAA, 2002). What this paper now intends to produce is evidence that these activities involve the learning of new sensio-motricities and that their development takes place in an emotionally charged environment.

Observations from the workshops

The observations that follow occurred between 2002–5, during which time the author was course leader for the BA in Applied Arts at Plymouth College of Art and Design, and also lectured on the FdA in Applied Arts. Both courses were supported by well-provisioned workshops dedicated to ceramics, glass, plasterworking, jewellery and large-scale metalwork.

The following observations are presented for analysis with an awareness that to some extent they fall short of the rigours expected of anthropological fieldwork. Participant-observation leans heavily towards the participant aspect and theoretical questions have been applied in retrospect. Though the examples could in isolation be considered fairly minor, expected occurrences or unremarkable, common sense conventions, their frequency and ubiquity raises important questions that form the foundations for productive future research, in a similar manner to Mauss's observations of trench digging and descending stairs in slippers.

During the period being discussed the author was placement mentor to a succession of PGCE students who, as part of their year long teaching placements, led practical workshops. Early attempts by the PGCE students at demonstrations of technical processes were frequently marred by their inability to draw the students' attention to how tactile, aural and visual feedback would help them undertake such activities successfully. As a consequence of debriefing discussions it became clear that whilst the PGCE students had mastered the relevant processes, most were not conscious of the feedback mechanisms they used to do so. Their ability to feel the resistance of the material being manipulated, either directly through the hands or via cutting or shaping tools, or to read the sounds made by the equipment or materials during the process, or the slight colour changes observed when heating or cooling materials were well developed, but not in a consciously intellectual sense. During the course of their placement each PGCE student had to learn to reflexively review their own actions, questioning how they controlled each process, before they could effectively teach the same processes to others.

A related problem occurred during the author's own experiences of teaching basic plaster mixing skills. This process involves mixing by hand precise amounts of powdered plaster and water that start to react after a few minutes, first thickening and then quickly becoming solid. The liquid mixture needs to be poured into moulds, where it sets, but if the mixture is poured too soon or too late the resulting solid plaster block is usually unsuitable for use. Recognising when the mixture is ready to pour only comes with practice, as the indications – a very slight warming of the mixture and increased viscosity – can only be felt by the person stirring the mixture; by the time the change is easily observable the mixture is unusable.

Describing the tactile feedback whilst demonstrating the process could only indicate to the students what they should be looking for when they undertook the same activity. Early student attempts at mixing frequently ended with a bucket of half-solid plaster and highly embarrassed students. When individual students could recognise at least one of the indications and therefore successfully complete the process they had immense trouble verbalising their new understanding to struggling and still frustrated friends. At this point any loss of complete concentration during the process would often still lead to a failed result. Eventually every student would learn how to command the basic process, and then it was possible to discuss how to manipulate the process further. Whilst it was possible to build on a student's phenomenological experience through subsequent discussions, it was not possible to give a student a full understanding of the basic process through speech alone. By the second year of the course all the students who had persisted in using plasterworking techniques could manage the process from start to finish whilst holding in-depth conversations, often only pausing when they sensed the mixture was ready and started pouring. However, they still found it difficult to describe to others how they knew the plaster mixture was in the right state to pour. The teaching of other manual techniques entailed similar phenomenological and emotional elements (and a growing nonchalance in practice): centring clay on the wheel, forging red-hot iron, keeping the glass mass centred on a blowing iron, and soldering, brazing and welding.

Observations of glassblowing classes provided evidence of the development of additional praxeological skills. Due to it being a communal activity involving handling a lump of very hot plastic material on the end of a long metal pole that needs to be kept in constant movement and manipulated before it cools, glassblowing requires a high level of teamwork. The team leader, called the chair, assumes authority and the chair's commands are accepted by the rest of the team without question. The chair often gives curt commands in a tone that in other situations would be considered socially unacceptable. Glassblowing as practiced in art and design colleges is little different from industrial glassblowing practice, the commonality being maintained through technicians' and lecturers' expectations and reconfirmed by demonstrations given by visiting lecturers and professionals from industry. Through observing demonstrations and their own practical experience in the glass shop, students learn the expected way behave and to manoeuvre round other workers, as well as the need to watch and follow the commands of the chair. It is remarkable that students whose behaviour in other situations can be challenging accept the distinctly hierarchical and structured interaction expected in a glass shop, even when they are continually in a low status situation, without complaint.

The observations above are replete with examples of different types of motricity. Plasterworking, throwing, blacksmithing, silversmithing and glassblowing all involve specific (though often similar) motor algorithms. In addition glassblowing could be seen as an exemplar (though not the only case) of sociometry, with motor communication an essential part of the process. The actions of the PGCE students and of the undergraduate students in plasterworking sessions indicate how learnt relevant sensorimotor skills quickly drop below the level of conscious thought.

Students, Staff and Subjectification

Having identified that the design practices under discussion do involve sensorimotor apprenticeships, we now need to consider if these activities are being undertaken in a sufficiently intense emotional context. The description of teaching basic plasterworking techniques included references to the immediate frustrations of students within the group, but undergraduate learning takes place within a much wider emotional context. Though each programme, and each student's experience within that programme, is different, general surveys of students' perceptions of their experience indicate that for over half of students education is undertaken against a background of highly significant and intertwining financial, relationship and time pressures, (Coxon, 2002; Kings College London Public Relations Department, 2007; Moore, 2002). Students are subject to a range of personal, familial and peer group expectations that contribute to their internal definitions of what constitutes achievement. The assessment grades awarded within and at the culmination of particular programmes contribute to these definitions and are particularly influential in encouraging comparisons within peer groups. Their role of grades in securing future employment opportunities, acceptance on higher level programmes, and success in applying for grants to support post-graduate study, make them appear incontrovertible evidence of attainment (or the lack of it). Assessment deadlines, formal critiques and evaluations and informal peer judgements (encouraged or otherwise) colour the lives, concerns, and actions of whole cohorts. Consequentially, it can be proposed that the conditions identified as necessary for praxeological subjectification exist within formal post-compulsory design education.

It is also important to recognise that far from being a blank slate, many students have already been through prior psychometric apprenticeships in emotional contexts, and have therefore also been subjected to praxeological subjectification before their arrival. Most design students entering post-compulsory education have had prior involvement with practical techniques related to design, including inputs as diverse as school technology and art and design classes, relatives' work activities, or a relative's or their own personal hobbies (Minahan & Cox, 2007; Ranson, 1989). In addition, particular towns or regions have historical relationships with individual artisan or craft disciplines and their continued practice can be an integral part of the social fabric and form a constant background to lived experience (Jones, 1996; Wise, 1949). Whilst in the UK many of the regional craft industries have dramatically declined in economic and social importance since the mid twentieth century, only retaining influence as elements of local heritage, in other parts of the world this is not the case and local craft technologies may be profoundly significant to the lives of international students (Campbell, 2002; Hoerig, 2003; Meredith, 1999; Sissons, 1993). It is also important to recognise that all these sociocultural circumstances will have been filtered through each individual learner's perceptions, including personal relationships with formal or informal teachers and mentors (who may or may not have been related to the learner), and localised perceptions of the status related to successfully practising particular techniques (Attfield, 2000; Hodge, 1967; Hoerig, 2003; Minahan & Cox, 2007; Rammell, 2004; Ranson, 1989).

Internalised symbolised experiences will dictate individual student's initial responses when they are reintroduced to the same activities in a design programme setting and their relationship to tasks that utilise those activities. Technical skill in undertaking a particular process does not necessarily equate with enthusiasm for that process. As responses are occurring at an emotional rather than intellectual level, students will also often be unable to articulate why they exhibit such a positive or negative response, or be aware this response has such a commanding influence over their behaviour. For educators managing programmes, this raises the question of whether the programme's introductory practical activities are sufficiently diagnostic to enable the lecturers delivering the sessions to identify such influences (assuming that the lecturers even have the experience and time to use the sessions for such a purpose). If not, as initial undergraduate assessment is usually criterion referenced rather than ipsative, it is possible it may be some distance into a course before the staff collectively identify that the distance travelled by an initially apparently talented student has been minimal or that a student is taking career forming decisions based on criteria very different from that of the lecturers.

The term subjectification was initially couched by Foucault in negative terms and can be considered a response to the assumption, widely held at the time of the publication of *Discipline and Punish*, that the modern era was one of freedom as opposed to earlier, more restrictive social systems (Foucault, 1979; Gutting, 2005). In the context being discussed it can be proposed that praxeological subjectification also has practical benefits and should be viewed as a phenomenon that enables individuals to construct an identity as a practitioner, an identity which can help support them when they face subsequent challenges in the later stages of their programme of study and professional career. Such a proposal, whilst purely conjectural, is circumstantially supported by the art and design QAA subject benchmark statement in its description of the necessary teaching and learning environments for HE art and design programmes:

> The dedicated studio-base rooms and individual workspaces that are typical of most providers of art and design HE, are highly valued by students and contribute substantially to their independence as learners. Access to high quality, capital intensive resources is equally valued. (QAA 2002, p.7, para 5.1.2)

It is interesting to note that the benchmark statement gives no indication as to why students find continual access to these resources so valuable. Though the studio-base rooms and workspaces are commonly considered as purely (expensive) functional resources, the statement does not contradict a reading that these environments also act as psychological supports for the students in the absence of lecturers, reinforcing a personal identification with the discipline through their role as appropriate arenas of performance for the practice of the relevant pyschomotric techniques.

It is not difficult to theorise why the discipline of glassblowing has developed and maintains a single set of sociomotric conventions, or why design education establishments follow these same conventions. Due to the nature of the process and material, poor communication results in complete failure, rather than an output of lower quality. This, and the physical risk incurred by miscommunication in such a potentially dangerous environment, has led to the need for widespread adoption of a single dominant glassblowing *habitus* by practitioners. The near universal adoption of this *habitus* has the additional benefit of supporting communality, enabling new teams to gel quickly and novices to more easily learn how they should behave. As a result, individuals can quickly form unified and focussed teams that can work effectively in a pressured and dangerous situation without the need for extensive prior or ad hoc negotiation.

Lastly it is also productive to consider a hitherto unremarked element of design education: the lecturing staff. Most design lecturers have become masters of at least one practical process, and many are skilled at wide variety encompassing different materials and sets of tools. During the course of developing this expertise lecturers have been subjected to the same processes of praxeological subjectification. As a consequence they frequently exhibit a strong psychological relationship (usually a positive one) to the practice and material culture of their chosen disciplines. But to what extent are lecturers aware of how this may influence their teaching practice? In much the same way as the novice teachers observed did not realise how they controlled a process, are experienced lecturers equally guilty of not realising the extent to which they expect students to identify with particular design disciplines in the same way and through the same practice as they themselves do? This problem is made more acute by the structure of many design courses which include a significant element of relatively separate textual design theory that promotes a set of diametrically opposed values; designers are described as isolated individuals who use intellectual decisions to impose their vision on materials, commanding techniques and processes as a necessary but malleable and neutral part of that activity. From this perspective, schools of communal practice are defined solely in terms of intellectual congruence, without any identification of solidarity through praxis. This approach interacts with and supports the post-industrial Western design industry, where celebrity designers are expected to create a personalised body of work in an identifiable style and the concept of individual intellectual copyright dominates practice. Students on such courses are torn between two competing and contradictory frameworks for constructing identity; one linguistic and theoretical, the other sensorimotor and practical.[2]

Conclusions

The elements identified as necessary for praxeological subjectification are in evidence in art and design education, and the observations described above can be used to support the contention that it is a significant feature of design students' learning. In addition, the same process exerts an influence over the behaviour of design lecturers. Though we talk of professionals as having mastered a discipline, it may be more correct to describe ourselves as becoming dominated by it, through our acceptance of its governmentality. This paper also proposes that praxeological subjectification is not negative or positive per se, but depends upon the circumstances and outcomes of its formation. Lecturers need to consider how far any student's previous development aligns or conflicts with the objectives of their programme in order to identify if it is acting as a barrier to learning or an educational support.

This discussion has concentrated on specific techniques of design involving materials with a long history of use, which could be defined as traditional craft disciplines. These were chosen due to historical circumstance, being disciplines the author was familiar with from personal practice and had observed during teaching. What remains to be established is how far the same processes occur wherever design practitioners engage with practical techniques and processes. Beyond the range of obvious practical specialist disciplines such as screenprinting, pattern-cutting, stoneworking, and cabinet-making, it is worth stating that more general design techniques such as drawing and CAD/CAM also involve instruments; instruments require manual techniques for use and manual techniques require psychometricity. The digital age has been prophesised to herald the end of manual production, but some commentators contend it is only generating new manual techniques that will replace or run alongside the old (Sennett, 2007). The rapid prototyping machine may eventually reorder our concepts of materiality, but a great deal of its operation and maintenance is currently closer to familiar practice than its advocates declare, or possibly even recognise. A productive avenue of inquiry would be to extend the breadth of design techniques under review, including those involving new technologies, in order to consider how far they replicate the features identified above.

Any identification of the existence and relative importance of praxeological subjectification in design practice, both generally and within specific design disciplines, relies on understanding what material culture does to subjects, rather than its conscious meanings for those subjects. I would envisage

---

2. A disparity between linguistic explanations and performative actions is not unique to this situation. Other examples are explored in Warnier's paper (2001, pp.17–19).

that to be effective research studies would need to follow a qualitative ethnographic methodology in order to not only record physical activities, including the subjects' levels of psychometricity (and when necessary for the task, sociometry), but also to relate these to the subjects' responses and their reactions to undertaking these same activities. As praxeological subjectification develops over time, there is a clear need for diachronic studies that identify common timescales and what circumstances cause variation in the speed of introjection, though large synchronic studies that looked at designers and design students who are at different stages of their education or practice may possibly also provide this information. In addition, the question of possible crucial formative periods and retention needs to be addressed. Does the process continually reinforce itself with continued practice? Or is it a case of there being a specific development period that subsequently retains a consistent level of influence? The answers to these questions would be of significant benefit to the teaching of design subjects, as well as being of theoretical interest.

Bibliography

Appadurai, A. (Ed.) (1986) *The Social Life of Things: commodities in cultural perspective* Cambridge, Cambridge University Press

Attfield, J. (2000) *Wild Things: The Material Culture of Everyday Life* Oxford & New York, Berg

Campbell, S. F. (2002) *The Art of Kula* Oxford/London, Berg

Coxon, K. (2002) A Degree of Stress <http://education.guardian.co.uk/students/story/0, 652350,00.html> 19/02/2002

Davies, M. W. (2005) *Introducing Anthroplogy* Cambridge, Icon Books

Eriksen, T. H. (2004) *What is Anthroplogy?* London, Pluto Press

Foucault, M. (1978) *The History of Sexuality, Volume 1: An Introduction* New York, Vintage

Foucault, M. (1979) *Discipline and Punish* Harnondsworth, Middlesex, Penguin

Gutting, G. (2005) *Foucault: A very Short Introduction* Oxford & New York, Oxford University Press

Hodge, W. (1967) 'Navaho Urban Silversmiths' in *Anthropological Quarterly*, Vol.40, No. 4, pp.185–200

Hoerig, K. A. (2003) *Under the Palace Portal: Native American artists in Santa Fe* Albuquerque, University of New Mexico Press

Jones, B. (1996) *Bill Jones' Notes from the Turning Shop* Lewes, East Sussex, Guild of Master Craftsmen Publications

Kings College London Public Relations Department, First National Study on Student Suicide <http://www.kcl.ac.uk/phpnews/wmview.php?ArtID=1742> 05/03/2007

Mauss, M. (2002) *The Gift* London, Routledge

Mauss, M. (2006) 'Techniques of the Body (1935)' in *Techniques, Technology and Civilisation*, N. Schlanger, (Ed.) New York/Oxford, Durkheim Press & Berghahn Books pp.77–95

Meredith, R. (1999) 'Art Education in Samoa: Acculturated identity' in *Art and Performance in Oceania*, B. Craig, B. Kernot, & C. Anderson, (Eds.) Honolulu, University of Hawaii Press pp.50–57

Minahan, S. & Cox, J. W. (2007) 'Stitch 'n Bitch: Cyberfeminism, a Third Place and the New Materiality' in *Journal of Material culture*, Vol.12, No.1, pp.5–21

Moore, W. Student Stress. <http://www.channel4.com/health/microsites/0-9/4health/stress/syp_student.html. 2002>

QAA (2002) *Subject Benchmark Statement for Art and Design* Gloucester, Quality Assurance Agency

Rammell, G. (2004) 'Goldsmith/Culturesmith' in *Bill Reid and Beyond: Expanding on Modern Native Art* K. Duffek & C. Townsend-Gault, (Eds.) Toronto/ Vancouver, Douglas and McIntyre, pp.44–58

Ranson, B. (1989) 'Craftwork, Ideology and the Craft Life Cycle' in *Journal of Design History*, Vol. 2, No. 2/3, pp.77–92

Sacks, O. (1986) *The Man Who Mistook His wife for a Hat* London, Picador

Schilder, P. (1935) *The Image and Appearance of the Human Body: Studies in the Constructive Energy of the Psyche* London, Keegan Paul

Schlanger, N. (1998) 'The Study of Techniques as an Ideological Challenge: Technology, Nation, and Humanity in the work of Marcel Mauss' in *Marcel Mauss: A Centenary Tribute*, W. A. A. N. J. James, (Ed.) New York & Oxford, Berghahn Books, pp.192–212

Sennett, R. (2008) *The Craftsman* London, Allen Lane

Sissons, J. (1993) 'The Systematisation of Tradition: Maori Culture as a Strategic Resource' in *Oceania*, Vol. 64, No. 2, pp.97–116

Warnier, J. P. (2001) 'A Praxeological Approach to Subjectification in a Material World' in *Journal of Material Culture*, Vol. 6, No. 1, pp.5–24

Wise, M. J. (1949) 'On the Evolution of the Jewellery and Gun Quarters in Birmingham' in *Transactions and Papers (Institute of British Geographers)*, Vol. 15, pp.59–72

Acknowledgements

Many thanks go to Michael Rowlands and Graeme Were for discussions during the initial stages of this paper, and an invitation to attend Richard Sennett's seminar on craftsmanship at UCL during a crucial stage of the paper's development. In addition I am indebted to Lynne Staley-Brookes and Tim Bolton at Plymouth College of Art and Design for agreeing to the inclusion of the educational observations that were drawn from my experiences at PCAD. Continued support from the SWLLN during the writing and presentation of this paper, in particular that of the SWLLN's Director, Belinda Payne, has been both welcomed and valued.

Chapter 4

Developing Research-Based Education:
A case study in teaching Interactive Digital Media Design

Tara Winters
Elam School of Fine Arts, University of Auckland

Introduction

The aim of this paper is to describe an approach to teaching and learning in art and design education that draws on the practices, processes and methodologies of research practice to effectively facilitate transformative learning. This work attempts to show how pedagogical research may be embedded into the practical teaching and learning experience, a leading theme of the Design and Pedagogy Conference where this work was presented in March 2007.

The paper outlines features of a third year undergraduate project unit in , Interactive Digital Media Design, designed to:

(a) facilitate a re-conceptualisation of the subject of study

(b) encourage a research-based engagement with the subject of study

(c) support the development of more sophisticated understandings of the nature, methods, and purposes of research in art and design

Context

Art and design degree courses at the Elam School of Fine Arts, The University of Auckland are research-based degree programmes, and as such, place an emphasis on interpreting, interrogating and experimenting with ideas, concepts and contexts. The challenge of designing a curriculum that effectively integrates research with learning presents itself in this teaching and learning context. Facilitating divergent approaches to art and design thinking and making, and encouraging risk-taking and the challenging of established ideas, conventions and models is a complex task for educators.

Research-based working methodologies seek to question, extend, invent and innovate, a central tenet being the *construction of new knowledge* (including the notion of knowledge new to *that* learner, and not necessarily new knowledge per se). Research approaches to subject learning contribute positively in critical ways to sound pedagogical aims concerning art and design education as the site where understandings of the nature of the subject of learning, and of conceptions of learning itself, are challenged and broadened.

In response to this challenge, this paper presents a case study at subject level describing an attempt to embed in the learning experience (at a philosophical as well as practical level) characteristics of a research based investigation drawing on pedagogical theories of transformative learning (Mezirow, 1991) and, particular to design pedagogy, learning and the design entity (Davies & Reid, 2001).

The study describes the rationale, ideas and methodology behind the design and delivery of a third year project unit titled 'Interactive Digital Media Design'. In answer to the challenge of aligning research with learning the approach centered on a number of ways of problematising the project to raise fundamental questions about the subject of study intended to promote a research style engagement. This included conceptualising the digital medium as unique, as a representational system for carrying ideas, information and concepts and prompting students to engage in alternatives that went beyond existing principles and conventions, through questioning where those principles and conventions derive from and reflecting on their usefulness as part of a progressive, research-driven approach to new media design.

Research and Teaching

In relation to the particular teaching and learning context at Elam School of Fine Arts, The University of Auckland, our Graduate Profile policy document states that 'an understanding and appreciation of the philosophical bases, methodologies and characteristics of scholarship, research, and creative work' is an attribute our graduates are expected to have developed (The University of Auckland Graduate Profile, 2003, s.1). Research-led teaching and learning practices are key practices within a research-led University. At curriculum level, the programme aims and objectives of the Bachelor of Fine Arts course clearly emphasise a focus on the development of research skills.

The nature of the relationship between teaching and research will be dependent on the discipline in question and the various methods, models and processes it accepts as research. Research culture in art and design is in a period of experimentation and development. Art and Design is at the beginning of the research process and debate is very much still in progress around the nature and value of design research, the basis on which practical studio work is recognised as research, and the problematic nature of defining what constitutes design knowledge. While it is not my intention here to contribute to the resolution of these long-standing issues, explaining the approach I have taken to the alignment of research with teaching and learning will touch on some aspects of these questions.

What constitutes research in the field of art and design may vary between individuals, and the particular relationship of teaching to research lies within an individuals teaching and research practice and how they conceptualise this relationship. Whilst acknowledging this it may still be useful to review common features of research in art and design and to use this information in planning effective research-led teaching and learning environments.

Research and art and design

The fluid nature of definitions of art and design, and the changing nature of its practices indicate the central role that research has in our field. Recognising that design is fundamentally about inquiry through its central acts of determining a situation for response and the formulation of a response that transforms an original situation helps one to appreciate the similarities in the processes of design and research. Design academic Professor Richard Buchanan describes definitions of design as serving 'strategic and tactical purposes in inquiry' (2001, p.8). Buchanan comments further that: 'a definition, whether formal or descriptive, is like a hypothesis in research: it gathers together what will be investigated and sets the relation of causes that will become the themes of subsequent inquiry' (1991, p.9). A questioning or testing of any single definition of design takes us immediately into the research process.

Similarly, design researcher Ken Friedman identifies questions as a central component of design research that generates new knowledge. Friedman offers a summary definition of research as being a 'way of asking questions' (2000, p.18), adding that 'all forms of research ask questions, basic, applied and clinical' (Friedman, 2000, p.18). The approach in this teaching unit involved proposing challenging questions about the nature of the digital medium, setting the starting point for inquiry around an important conceptual understanding of the subject of study that supported exploratory and experimental modes of engagement characteristic of research investigations. The subject of study was presented as an area for discovery rather than a fixed category with established rules and conventions. This represented a shift in emphasis from drawing on established conventions in order to 'problem solve' in this domain, to the consideration of the potential as well as the limitations of the digital medium as a revolutionary *new* medium in the communication of ideas and information.

Degrees in art and design are practice-based. For many artists and designers research indicates practice. The concept of practice-based research is key to understanding the nature and forms of research in art and design and is an important discussion for future researchers in the field to be familiar with. Research is communicated via work exhibited, and through objects, systems, performances, and events facilitated or created.

Christopher Frayling (1993/94) identifies several classes of research in art and design. Included in Frayling's descriptions is a class of research *through* art and design, a kind of action-based research model where the process and results of art and design itself constitute the means by which research is carried out and through which the results are communicated. John Danvers (2003) describes practice-based research as: 'Arising from particular needs and purposes, knowledge is gained and externalized through a continuous process of finding out, trying out and making, within a framework of critical reflection and contextualization' (Danvers, 2003, p.55). Darren Newbury points out in a journal article titled 'Knowledge and Research in Art and Design' that 'what becomes apparent is that it is characteristic of research in art and design that it is motivated by art and design practice. Whether it is research in industrial design or in fine art, the application of knowledge is often at the forefront of the research' (Newbury, 1996, p.219). Frayling's, Danvers' and Newbury's descriptions help us to conceptualise practice-based models of research in art and design, models we see our students working to when they develop and test ideas, processes, and contexts through experimental, exploratory, and connective modes of practical inquiry.

The approach taken in this studio project encouraged students to develop more sophisticated conceptions of what constitutes research in art and design. Students were encouraged to move beyond a conceptualisation of research as the gathering and organising of information to regarding this as just one activity involved in research. The potential for artifacts to embody the results of research and present information/ideas used to develop work (reflecting the iterative nature of the design process) contributed to transforming prior conceptions of the nature and purpose of research in the learning process and how research can be conducted and communicated through the practice of art and design.

The following table attempts to summarise the relationship of features of research in art and design to the research-based learning model developed for the project unit in interactive media design.

Table I: Features of Research Processes in Art and Design and their relationship to the Research-Based learning model used to teach Interactive Digital Media Design.

Research Processes in Art and Design	Relationship to research based learning in undergraduate project unit (Interactive Digital Media Design)
Map area for investigation and set project aims and objectives: Describe phenomena to be examined/explored, specify key questions, establish parameters for the investigation.	Challenge proposed to students: 'What opportunities does the representation of information and ideas in an interactive multimedia environment that consists of objects, relationships and events offer to the pursuit of enriching our experiences with content?'
Become familiar with current approaches, similar projects and existing practices of relevance. This includes considering unconventional approaches and actively seeking connections and links that may inform research in surprising ways.	Students are asked to consider the application of conventions established for older modes of communication (particularly print-based) to new media environments. Process of gathering and reflecting on existing examples of new media art and design works and questioning how appropriate this practice is.
Active inquiry toward the production of original work. Process of discovery through interacting with new ideas, media and processes. Exploring alternatives, establishing new connections, testing, revising.	Generating ideas, developing concepts, exploring the potentials of the medium. Creative play and experimentation, imaginative exploration (being open to unexpected outcomes, accidents, chance events). Questioning one's own pre-existing knowledge and understanding of the digital medium.
Critical analysis and evaluation. Drawing conclusions with reference to original project aims and objectives. This may involve revisiting any previous stage – iterative process.	Students are encouraged to critically reflect on the ways they have/have not utilized the properties, attributes and characteristics of the medium in the effective communication of information and ideas. This informs changes in one's personal conception of the subject of study (a sense and meaning-making experience). The construction of new knowledge for that learner (*not* necessarily new knowledge per se). Development of new personal understanding through critical inquiry.
Practice-led research model. Knowledge is tested and advanced through 'doing'. Practical testing and application of knowledge is a leading activity.	Presentation of research activity is in the form of practical experiments with digital media.
Art and design outcomes constitute the vehicle for communicating research results. Forms of presentation of the research are appropriate to the subject of the research. Relates to Christopher Frayling's (1993/94) category description of research *for* art and design where results of the research are embodied in art/design outcomes as opposed to verbal or written accounts of results.	Presentation of the results of research are embodied within artifacts/products. Students become familiar with the ways in which knowledge is presented and contested in the field of art and design *through* art and design outcomes.
Contingent nature of knowledge in subject area and fluid nature of subject definitions. Definitions support researchers in clarifying the directions of the work/themes of inquiry rather than provide final answers.	Realisation that views, theories and opinions are always subject to change. Understanding that lack of a final or single definition contributes in positive ways to researched based inquiry in the field of art and design (Buchanan, 2001).

Teaching for Conceptual Change (transformative learning)

Students hold differing conceptions of the nature of the subject of study and what learning in that subjects consists of. In a design education study that asked whether the experience of learning and teaching in design education, both for students and teachers, is consistent with conceptions shared within the educational community about the professional world of designers Davies & Reid report noticing 'a direct relation, in many cases, between students' conceptions of, and approaches to, learning' (2001, p.180). At higher conceptual levels, Davies & Reid describe a group of students who have a highly sophisticated view of the subject of study (design).

Davis & Reid go on to discuss familiar teaching methodology in design education, including project-based learning, in relation to the results of their research:

> On the basis of the research, it would appear that project-based learning will only be successful if the project is designed to develop the student's construction of the design entity as well as promoting learning at the higher conceptual levels. If the project is not designed to challenge students in this way then those students who conceive of learning as teacher-focused and skill based will continue to do so. Problematising the project, on the other hand, positions students to question both their conception of design (the design entity) and how they should go about learning design. (Davis & Reid, 2001, p.182)

Assignment design can be intentionally focused on complicating students' notions of the subject of study. Ill-structured or 'wicked problems' in design have pedagogical advantages in this sense because they are associated with uncertainty and ambiguity, and require open-ended, experimental, reflexive approaches that challenge easy interpretation, and are receptive to unexpected outcomes, qualities inherent in research-based investigation. By requiring students to wrestle with ideas and interpret situations, by presenting challenging, indeterminate project briefs, a deep approach to learning is encouraged that supports personal constructions of new knowledge.

Fost describes wicked design problems as:

> ... the sources of lifelong investigation, the wells from which we draw again and again, the nodes from which we spring into research and to which we return to try out new ideas. They might, in fact, not be recognized as problems at all. On the trail of a wicked problem, artifacts represent waypoints rather than solutions. (Fost, 2004, p.10)

Problematising this project in Interactive Media Design began with a questioning approach to the relationship of information, ideas and concepts, and the mediums, codes, and systems used to represent them. Compare the scope of the project prompt 'Design a website for ...' with the question 'What opportunities does the representation of information in a digital, multimedia, interactive environment that consists of objects, relationships and events offer to the pursuit of enriching our experiences with content'? The latter sets the scope of inquiry at a higher conceptual level, encouraging students to reflect at an early stage on the representational system being used to communicate information. Students are prompted to engage experimentally with the mode of communication while developing ideas about the effective communication of content.

A project brief of this nature sets the scene without prescribing the result, calling for an exploratory approach with the digital medium. It invites us to think about technological change and its impact on the systems and languages we use to represent the world. By pointing to such fundamental issues it represents a 'well from which we draw again and again' (Fost, 2004, p.10) and by facilitating a re-conceptualisation of the medium of communication encourages a more sophisticated view of the subject of study.

Research based inquiry involves experimenting with new ideas and approaches to develop ones personal conceptions of a subject. Framing the project brief in a critical, questioning manner that raises issues beyond the remit of the particular investigation at hand supports students in advancing their understanding of the larger area within which the current investigation lies.

A critical approach to the study of new media design will raise issues surrounding technological advancement in relation to the contemporary communications environment and point to more fundamental questions such as: have digital, interactive technologies been responsible for a fundamental shift in the means by which we communicate? What is the nature of digital, interactive communications? This fundamental questioning about the nature of the medium, its effects and creative potentials, provides fertile ground for students to respond through making, reflecting and evaluating – through research. It also connects the idea that the results of research investigations usually raise new questions and suggest new directions, problems or opportunities as often as they resolve particular issues.

A superficial investigation may stop when a known 'formula' or familiar solution is found to satisfy project goals, for example, the use of a familiar interface metaphor to access web content. But when problems contain complex ideas and questions different working methodologies and approaches are called for – research-based approaches. 'Wicked' new media design problems may require a critique of existing interface metaphors, and responses can contribute to the developing languages and theories of a revolutionary communications technology.

An example of student work can provide an illustration in relation to these ideas. Study at studio three level of the Bachelor of Fine Arts degree at Elam School of Fine Arts, the University of Auckland, aims to develop a deeper understanding of the notion of research as an open-ended, critical and reflexive activity. Students are encouraged to engage with research methodologies in art and design in the generation and ongoing development of a personal research-based practice.

In response to this educational context third year student Kentaro Yamada undertook an investigation into interface design which challenged existing models of human-computer interaction. Working at the cross-roads of art and design, Yamadas' approach to a direct manipulation user interface design combines a graphical representation of system objects that relate to real world objects. The system (developed using Macromedia Flash software using the Action Script programming language) allows a user to interact directly with a graphic representation of a dandelion bud in ways that are analogous to how one would interact with its real world counterpart.

An image of a dandelion is triggered into action by users interacting with a physical device set in front of a projected graphic – a microphone mounted on a stand. Users are able to 'blow' the seeds of the dandelion bud through the microphone, which causes the on-screen image to update. The system is sensitive to more or less force; blowing harder or more softly into the microphone affects the image differently.

'Tampopo' is a sophisticated integration of graphic, sound, animation, and interactive elements that create a unique user-experience. The representational devices selected, and the ways in which they are used, effectively establish an analogy to the real world object, setting an immediately intuitive context for user participation. User anticipation and expectation is rewarded when the system responds in a predictable and satisfying way via graphic, audio and moving image components that update and change in response to user input. Questioning the nature of human-computer interaction through practical experimentation the project represents a critical as well as explorative engagement with the medium for communication, specifically here in relation to the audience experience of interacting with a digital system.

Fig. 1. Installation Documentation of: 'Tampopo Project' on site at 'rm 103 Gallery', Auckland, New Zealand, June 2005

Fig. 2. Installation Documentation of: 'Tampopo' on site at 'rm 103 Gallery', Auckland, New Zealand, June 2005.

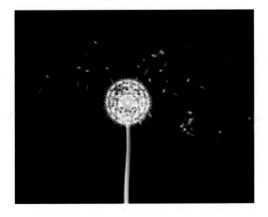

Fig. 3. Still screen grab of 'Tampopo Project'

Conclusion

In this paper I have outlined an approach to teaching and learning Interactive Digital Media designed to align research with learning at undergraduate level. I have attempted to demonstrate how integral the processes and practices of research are to teaching and learning for conceptual change.

Research-led teaching and learning practices, which draw on the idea that just as research is an integral part of art and design practice it can also be the site of effective teaching and transformative learning, is considered here as central to a perceptive response to contemporary conditions in the field of design education. These conditions include: the rise of critical design practices; moves to contextualise graphic design as an open-ended intellectual pursuit; and the rise of design practices concerned with contextual experimentation that 'question not so much the form of design, but the possibilities of its practice' (Blauvelt, 2003 p.40).

Bibliography

Blauvelt, A. (2003) 'Towards Critical Autonomy or Can Graphic Design Save Itself?' *Émigré*, No. 64 Winter, pp.35–43

Buchanan, R. (2001) 'Design Research and the New Learning' *Design Issues*, Vol. 17, No. 4, Autumn pp.3–23

Danvers, J. (2003) 'Towards a Radical Pedagogy: Provisional Notes on Learning and Teaching in Art and Design *International Journal of Art & Design Education*, Vol. 22 ,No. 1 pp.47–57

Davies, A. & Reid, A. (2001) 'Uncovering Problematics in Design Education: Learning and the Design Entity' Swann, C. & Young, E. (Eds) *Proceedings of the International Conference: Re-Inventing Design Education in the University, December 11–13, 2000*, Perth Australia Curtin University School of Design pp.178–184

Fost, M. (2004) 'Dead Animals: Considerations Toward and Expanded Practice in Graphic Design'n *Future History, AIGA Design Education Conference, October 16–17, 2004, Chicago, Illinois*. Available from: <http://futurehistory.aiga.org/> (12/11/2004)

Frayling, C. (1993/94) 'Research in Art and Design' in *Royal College of Art Research Papers*, Vol. 1, No.1 pp.1–5

Friedman, K. (2000) 'Creating design knowledge: from research into practice' in *IDATER Conference Proceedings, Loughborough University, England*. Available from: <http://www.lboro.ac.uk/departments/cd/docs_dandt/idater/downloads00/Friedman2000.pdf> (12/11/2004)

Newbury, D. (1996) 'Knowledge and research in art and design' *Design Studies*, Vol. 17, No. 2 pp.215–219

Mezirow, J. (1991) *Transformative Dimensions of Adult Learning* San Francisco, Jossey-Bass

University of Auckland (2003) The University of Auckland Graduate Profile, The University of Auckland, New Zealand, [Internet]. Available at: <http://www.auckland.ac.nz/uoa/for/currentstudents/careerplanning/finding/gradprof.cfm>

Acknowledgement

Many thanks to Kentaro Yamada, studio three student (2005) at the Elam School of Fine Arts, The University of Auckland, for allowing the author to discuss and reproduce examples of studio coursework.

Design Codes and Design Language

Eleni Tracada
University of Derby

Introduction

Before any reference to my teaching experience, it should be timely to talk about my own learning experience; this could explain how and why I have been inspired to pursue studies, practise and finally teach design and architecture. I studied architecture in the Faculty of Florence in Italy between 1973 and 1980; I moved there from Greece during the last year of the colonel's regime, which lasted from 1967 for seven very tough years for everybody, and especially for students. So, as happened to a large number of students in Greece, I had to struggle to get enough preparatory studies at a standard which could offer me the chance to look at more developed systems in higher education abroad. Therefore, beyond the material offered at high school level, I had to search for other private tuition schools in order to be able to learn and practise drawing and also learn more about the history of art, design and architecture.

In the early 1970s I managed to gain access to the Eliades School of Arts and Drawing in Athens and there I started eagerly learning arts and drawing under the attentive guidance of Kostas Eliades, one of the most well-known maestros in Greece and France. In fact, Kostas Eliades' had attended the Ecole des Beaux Arts of Paris before World War II; he had not only been my first inspiring teacher of drawing, but also he introduced me and the rest of the class to the years of exciting creativity in literature, arts, design and architecture in Europe just in the middle of the horrors of two world wars. Eliades did not use to teach by means of elaborate presentations as we are used to today. Instead he used to talk and recall his own days as a student, learning and training under other maestros in France. Therefore, our imagination had to play a vital role in learning. Besides his narrative, Eliades used to read the poetry and prose of famous authors. Whilst drawing, the words were unconsciously translated into powerful lines, shapes and forms by combinations of patterns of colours. The year I spent in Eliades' School of Drawing had been a milestone in my career development as a professional architect and later teacher; my skills in drawing and designing were further enhanced by the teaching and support of another architect at the same school. Timos Missios [1] taught us architectural drawing through

---

1. In 1972 Timos Missios also started teaching in the famous Vakalò School of Arts and Design in Athens, in which he is now one of its directors.

historical explorations of existing buildings and open spaces around Athens; we discovered how to read the historical past life of the built environment.

Consequently, the accomplishment of learning how to be creative was enriched by further studies in architecture in the Faculty of Architecture in Florence, Italy. At the end of these studies and before moving to Britain, I had been practising as a self-employed architect in Florence between 1983 and 1993. Between 1993 and 1996, I pursued MA studies in 3D and Interior Design at Manchester Metropolitan University where I had the great opportunity to have Professor John Parkinson-Bailey, historian, as one of the supervisors of my thesis; he also inspired me to choose a teaching career in higher education.

Aspirations and context

In this paper I wish to explain my intentions and experience as a teacher involved with ongoing research in spatial design teaching, with particular reference to my own teachers' teaching on social architecture and inclusive societies during my years in Italy. This paper will additionally explain how co-ordination of research between teachers and students may lead from codes and modelling to concepts and philosophies and finally to syntax and design language in order to attain coherent, creative and innovative solutions. I shall make reference to learning and teaching outcomes from specific projects developed in interior architecture recently and personal experiences in developing research in history and theories of architecture.[2] And above all, I should like to reflect on my own practice as an educator by critically looking back on my own history of formation.

Education and practice in architecture has seen a dramatic development in many European countries after World War II, but the origins of the educational structure in modern architecture can be found in Italy's more tumultuous years back in the 1930s, when architects managed to impose 'law and order' in their first Schools of Architecture and also declared their independence from the oppressive establishment of engineering cliques, such as these of the School of Engineering in Milan or the traditionalist and conservative Academies of Arts in Rome and Milan. Back in the 1930s, Italian architects such as Giovanni Michelucci[3] managed to create strategies and won competitions under Mussolini's repressive regime. Politics became a vital part of Italian architecture and revolutionary Modernist ideas flourished under the constant threat of the Fascist regime. Nothing was able to stop Rationalism[4] and Mussolini himself had to declare a status of acceptance of the architects' rules, until Nazism prevailed in Italy in the late 1930s and war stopped any activity everywhere in Europe. Whereas

---

2. I started teaching Interior Design to students at distance learning at the Open College of Arts, Barnsley in 1999. Between October 2001 and May 2007, I taught Interior Design at Leeds College of Art and Design to Year 2 and 3 students and supervised project work and dissertations. Currently I am teaching Studio Design 1, History of Art, Design and Architecture, Innovations in Design and Technology and I am supervising Independent Studies' Projects in the Department of Built Environment, Faculty of Arts, Design and Technology of the University of Derby.

3. Giovanni Michelucci (1891–1990), born in Pistoia in Tuscany, was a famous Italian architect working and dealing for many years with public works related to mainly social architecture. Michelucci worked as a teacher in the Faculty of Architecture of Florence from the 1930s (when the Faculty emerged) until 1948 when he moved to the Faculty of Engineering of Bologna until the late 1950s. Then he carried on working on projects until the end of his life; he founded a Foundation bearing his own name which is still working on unfinished project work or on projects inspired by his ideas on supporting local communities, mental health and reformation institutions and other projects of public interest.

4. Rationalism was the term used to distinguish design and architecture during the Modernist era in Italy between 1920s and 1930s; the term emerged for the first time in the title of an exhibition of design and architecture in Rome in the 1920s. Between the followers of this movement we can find names like Antonio Sant'Elia, Giuseppe Pagano, Giuseppe Terragni, etc.

Modernists from Germany's Bauhaus School were escaping to Britain and America, Italian architects were defiant towards Fascism; they stayed in their schools and unions and continued to produce designs which managed to be recognized as archetypes for further developments in Postmodernism after the end of World War II.

The Faculty of Architecture in Florence at which I studied in the 1970s had emerged during the turbulent years of Fascism under the guidance of architects like Giovanni Michelucci, and it survived the war to see its new programme develop soon after. This new programme was the result of discussions and debate between architects and teachers who had taught in the Faculty for many years. I had the opportunity to be taught by most of these innovative educators. In the Faculty I learnt about my profession and techniques to maintain an active interest in innovation in research and continuous investigation into social and political issues related to design and architecture. Although Giovanni Michelucci left the Faculty of Architecture in the 1960s, he always kept contact with teachers and students until the last years of his life; he has been considered one of the main promoters of liberal programmes in architecture and also a skilled educator of many generations of architects until his death, just two days before the celebrations of his centenary birthday, in December 1990. I had the opportunity to meet Michelucci on various occasions and also had been involved with activities promoted by the Michelucci Foundation and the Regional Council of Tuscany for many years until very recently.[5]

Following the passing of my teachers, I worked as a professional for a decade in Florence (before moving in Britain in 1993) and pursued continuous independent research whilst in practice. Drawing for me became synonymous with creative research and architectural history blended with the architect and researcher, as has always happened to my teachers as well. My main ambition has been to transfer my skills and values to my students and my efforts have been repaid by the end, as you will see in this paper. Being a student in the 1970s, it was inevitable for me to be involved in activities related to cutting edge methods of teaching of architects, like Adolfo Natalini,[6] founder of the Superstudio group. In the years of revolution in the Faculty, Superstudio also collaborated with other groups, such as Archizoom, founded by Andrea Branzi.[7] So, radical architecture has had a particular effect on me and most of the radical architecture's values still remain evident in my teaching.

---

5. In July and August 2000, The Regional Council of Tuscany in Florence and the Michelucci Foundation (Via Beato Angelico 15, S. Domenico, Fiesole, Italy) organised a Campus in various cities; I worked in a team of twenty-nine experts from several countries aiming to produce a Charter on housing and urban integration of immigration in Tuscany. Special publications came out from this Campus, such as Nicola Solimano, Antonio Tosi (ed.s) (2000), *Living in City and Urban Cultures*, Florence: Ed. Polistampa.

6. Adolfo Natalini was born in Pistoia in 1941. 'After a pictorial experience, that shall be reflected in his constant use of drawing, he took a degree in Florence in 1966 and founded Superstudio (with Cristiano Toraldo di Francia, Gian Piero Frassinelli, Roberto and Alessandro Magris). Since 1979 Natalini started his own activity and focalised his research about the project in historical centres in Italy and Europe, looking for the traces time puts on objects and places and proposing a conciliation between collective memory and private memory.' (Ibelings, 2003, back cover page)

7. Andrea Branzi, architect and designer, was born in Florence in 1938 where he was awarded a degree in architecture in 1967; he lives and works in Milan. Between 1964 and 1974, he had been a member of the group Archizoom Associati; several original pieces of work of projects of that famous radical group are held by the Centre of Studies and Archives on Comminication of the University of Parma and the Centre Georges Pompidou in Paris. He is a very active teacher (associated professor in the Faculty of Architecture and Industrial Design of the Polytechnic of Milan) and designer in experimental industrial design, architecture and urban planning.

Genesis of radical architecture and teaching

In the 1970s Archizoom, an avant-garde group of Florentine architects, affirmed that 'ultimate purpose of the modern architecture is the eradication or elimination of the architecture itself' (Navone, et al., 1974, p.7). However, during the same years and because of general mistrust towards all previous education systems, most architects believed that every single model of urban form had failed. In 1974, by reflecting back on the years of student uprising, Andrea Branzi affirmed that it was generally thought that urban planning had become part of some sort of 'institutional instrumentalism', because 'Urbanism'[8] used to be imposed by law; he expressed his strong criticism by saying that 'urban planning may be enforced by the use of weapons in the years to come ahead' (Navone, et al., 1974, p.8).

In fact, urban planning should use correct policies related to urban areas and it should be accepted by society as a discipline, understanding clearly all manifestations of architecture in it; architecture is thought of as a non-political tool. According to the philosophy of the 1970s, architecture should always verify the social values of all operations set by urban planning. In the years before the student revolution, architects thought that urban planning had never aspired to offer equilibrium; particularly in the 1970s, architects and students thought that no moments of equilibrium ever existed. Between the 1950s and 1970s, in Italy we could find local authorities asking architects and planners to reduce the dimensions of their projects into the format of very simple physical models in scale, and the model became the real alternative to all processes of verification.

In the 1970s, many avant-garde groups adopted some methods of traditional presentation combined with new methods of the so-called 'Linguistic Metabolism'. But, according to the radical groups, architecture ought to embrace technology and show its technological metabolism in a different, figurative way. Models of high technological concept were made of collages of machinery parts and organic materials; they could honestly represent an organic architectural environment and create clarity in visual communication. Everything was left free to open research and continuous investigation and, as young students, we all had to adapt our activities in line with new historical rules imposed by new teaching methods. So, Utopia exists in the real process of a project and cannot be imposed by policies and regulations. Architecture can be a metaphor and a real natural phenomenon at the same time.

In the 1970s architects discovered a new way of doing architecture and did not intend to create only housing and commercial buildings. Architects discovered that architecture did also mean expression, communication and innovation; they recognised the fact that, by separating creativity from construction, they were able to explore more concepts and ideas as a means of primary motivation. Radical architecture was now able to identify key relationships between users and the natural environment. Therefore, architects could now work by following new social models of culture and had to practise according to newly introduced social cultures; that meant that whole communities were able to reclaim their creative power as one of their main civil rights. Everybody could challenge the intellectual class in order to become an author themselves.

The adventure of the new avant-garde architecture started in Florence between 1963 and 1967 inside cultural and ideological debates, was promoted by the most up-to-date cultural movements of students. New teachers in Florence, like Leonardo Savioli and Leonardo Ricci, proposed experimental programmes of studies and new methods of teaching. The titles of taught subjects now included

---

8. Urbanism is the study of cities and it is related to the notion of creating and designing cities according to local communities needs and necessities; Urbanism in Italian Faculties of architecture became a strong subject which has linked architecture with policy making at a local and national level. So, Urbanism has been always interested in the geographic, economic, political, social and cultural environment of cities and the imprint of all these forces on the built environment.

Fig.1. Natalini architetti: Boscotondo at Helmond (1995–2000) – a small paved square with Roberto Barni's bronze sculptures. (Source: Ibelings, H. (2003) 'A Dutch Perspective on the Dutch architecture of Adolfo Natalini', in *Adolfo Natalini: Album Olandese* Florence: Aión Edizioni, p.55)

'Integrated Urban Planning', 'Visual Design' and 'Spaces of Social Participation'. The profile of the architect was now considered as a positive image dealing with primary social problems and the architectural design was inspired by intellectual creativity. The component of creative imagination was enhanced by the use of technological imagery. As young architects we had the opportunity to come across contemporary works produced by other colleagues in Vienna and London. In one of his articles in the review *Casabella*, Andrea Branzi had mentioned that the Archigram should be considered as our 'ancestors of current research activities in architecture' (Branzi, 1972 p.2).

As young architects in Florence, we were familiar with all innovators very well, since the Vallecchi Editori, famous Florentine publishers, had translated and published Ulrich Conrad's *Manifesti e programmi per l'architettura del XX secolo* (Manifestos and Programmes of Twentieth Century Architecture) in which several new manifestos represented a clear denial of Rationalism. Between 1960 and 1963, students in Italy were also influenced by famous Italian architects like Giovanni Michelucci, who used to experiment with model-making by using organic materials in order to explain amazing sculptural and exceptionally technological buildings. Pop Art and culture also emerged and became a field of cultural reference for revolutionary students during the same years. Pop Art had changed the image of new culture in architecture; architecture was now represented as a *global image*. The experience of Pop Art was imported into the society of young Florentine architects and students of architecture mainly by Adolfo Natalini, who used to work closely with Roberto Barni, sculptor (fig. 1), and Gianni Ruffi, an artist. The three of them formed the so-called School of Pistoia (Pistoia has been always a thriving city in arts, culture and architecture since the 1920s and it was promoted by the Modernist movement). Pistoia also became famous before this due to Giovanni Michelucci, leader of the Gruppo Toscano,[9] who had won the competition for the design of the Railway Station of Florence, one of the finest examples of Modernist architecture in the 1930s.

Adolfo Natalini came from a traditionally radical environment and introduced Pop Art as a medium of architectural visual communication. The Pop Art illustration method was soon adopted by many young architects as we saw in the exhibitions with the title *Superarchitettura* (Super Architecture) in Pistoia in 1966 and in Modena in 1967. In their Manifesto presented on that occasion, the student architects declared in a prophetic way:

> Superarchitettura is the architecture of Super production, of Super consumerism, of Super induction to consumerism, to the Supermarkets, to Superman and to Super petrol. (Excerpt translated from the Manifesto/Poster of the 2nd Exhibition of Superarchitettura, 1967).

---

9. Giovanni Michelucci and the Gruppo Toscano (a group of his students at that time) won the competition for the Railway Station of Florence which was built in 1933 and it is thought to be one of the most important architectural examples of Modernism in Italy.

Here the intention is not only sarcastic, but also demystifying; there is confidence that the users can finally rise up against consumerism. Now architecture is intended to resolve both urban and human problems at the same time.

Today, Adolfo Natalini is an established professor in the Faculty of Architecture in Florence. I interviewed him in his studio in Florence on 30 April 2004. During that interview, Natalini strongly denied that architecture had ever been in decline; instead he affirmed that architecture is still alive, or better, architecture is still in evolution. Adolfo Natalini's work is a clear answer. In his small sketchbooks, the so-called *tacuini*, we can find sketches created by the same techniques used in the Superstudio's *istogrammi* (webs); he is still trying to compare 'generating' webs of lines hidden in the main structure and the façades or external skins of buildings.

By referring to Natalini's work (see fig. 1), Hans Ibelings, Dutch architectural historian, affirms that architecture cannot be eradicated or dormant; non-built Superstudio projects are still valid research patrimony for younger generations. Ibelings affirmed that there is 'a mechanism in architectural criticism and history whereby everything is constantly repeated and everything and everybody is forever being compared with their earlier selves' (Ibelings, 2003, p.7). In Natalini's work, webs grown inside the urban fabric of Tuscan towns, and especially in Pistoia, have managed to become powerful lines of architectural design and style. Because of these lines, which are infinite and in continuous motion, architecture remains constantly in motion and evolving. No place is similar to another, but there is a common link between places. Architecture is an explosion of lines intended to accompany human life manipulated by architects and their own creativity.

Eternal drama of lines in architectural drawing

Any line has been always an inspirational element into our work as architects and researchers. During my practising years I also had the opportunity to research urban patterns of regeneration in historical city fabrics; I also carried on researching and discovering interesting findings which can show us why cities are developing in a very organic way, in which human energy plays a vital role. Hidden pathlines in urban fabric can be often considered as urban indexes of human behaviour; they can prove and also guarantee continuous and harmonious development at all times. I pursued research on urban developments for many years and gradually discovered it to be supported by strong evidence through various authors' work, from maths to arts.

Pathways drawn through landscapes and contained by urban fabric may be considered powerful elements of uninterrupted urban development in every town and city around the globe.

How can human beings who are motivated by emotions be so <u>rational</u> to follow lines and also perform along these powerful elements in such an intensive manner that art and architecture can spiral out of them at any moment of everyday life? Every single person can be an artist or <u>performer</u> capable to orchestrate a cosmic movement of pathlines exploding into cosmic geometries which can penetrate nature and create artefacts; this is the perpetual way of creating three dimensional forms in harmony with human deeds or activities or actions. In that eternal play, a human being unconsciously is transformed into an <u>actor</u> or <u>performer</u> or <u>art-doer</u> or finally an <u>artist</u>. (Tracada, 1996)

Artists have been always inspired by geometric forms without being mathematicians; mathematics is intellectual and verbal, whilst art is made of emotions and is non-verbal. Guillaume Apollinaire's famous quote from *The Cubist Painters* affirming that 'geometry is to the plastic arts what grammar is to the art of the writer' (Apollinaire, 1970, p.13) may be considered strong evidence as to the indexical character of complex geometries, such as grids created by intersecting dynamic lines, for example. Therefore, the reality is that we have all been fascinated by geometries made by generating lines as mystical forces able to create primordial cells or forms; form comes to the real world when line moves along a creative performing process. There is always an everlasting performance act of lines which penetrates space and defines it as a *telic* art.

Line as *proforma* (performance) especially in pictorial spaces has been the main procreating element in the arts. Also in architecture, performing lines have been generously manipulated by architects in order to create spaces. It is obvious that lines could affect our intentions of creating at any time; cities are made of infinite vertical and horizontal lines. Lines do not only form edges, boundaries and outlines, but also penetrate whole spaces as path-generators of buildings. Therefore, arts and urbanism have simply emerged during this 'eternal act of the line performance act' (Tracada, 1996). And because *act* means *action,* it becomes obvious that complexity in systems of actions can discharge enormous amounts of performing or procreating energy to create complex artefacts, such as buildings and cities.

The glossary provenance of performance's meaning relates to the verb *perform* and *-ance*, in Anglo-French, and its main meaning is the action of performing. The presence of the component *form*, as a physically powerful element of the whole composite word, may be the key indexical meaning transferred into arts and architecture by means of real scales in artistic and architectural compositions. This assumption may become more congruous, if we also consider the etymological sense recommended by the dictionary as follows: 'to carry through in due form' (*The Oxford English Dictionary*, 1989, p.123).

Performance or *proforma* can be the whole mystic process which precedes the formation or genesis of forms. We cannot avoid the meaning of the Latin word proforma; proforma means *to form in front of* or before and this may associate proforma (or performance) to space, as time and place. Artists can juxtapose spaces and elements to increase interaction and finalise a diverse *telic act* of performance. As a matter of fact, forming a space by forms through human participation is a very complex act, because of different 'codes' and 'conventions' dictated by individual human emotions able to empower manipulation of human behaviour. Therefore, in this innate environment called the space of 'line performance act', the artist, or better, the *performer* moves, creates and lives in it.

Line, performance and act connected together may become key codes; act is a performance of an intelligent being. The formal etymology of the word *act* may be equally interesting and important as that of performance; the meaning of act becomes fascinating if we explore its primordial roots in time. We can discover that *act* presents a solid bond to the ancient Arian root *ak-* or *ak(c)-*is, as also accounted in the Old Greek language. This root contains the real original meaning of a very sharp edge or of a pointing and intimidating (or piercing and penetrating) element. If we regard act and action as penetrating elements into a space, we may be able at some point to define a specific space according to these co-ordinates; they turn out to be scale co-ordinates of an old index showing developments of human behaviour in different places around the world. Whenever we explore that magnificent performing act of an explosion of lines into the natural environment (concept), at the same time we discover and define its genesis, consistency and affinity and, most importantly, its boundaries inside the built environment (syntax and design language).

According to the vocabulary, act is 'a state of accomplished fact or reality, as distinguished from subjective existence, intention' (*The Oxford English Dictionary*, 1989, p.123). A subjective intention relates to a subject or to a practitioner of act as art; that means it relates to an architect. An action or performance act presumes the active presence of a human being or a group of human beings and, therefore, by exploring 'act-art', we discover the complexity and the plurality of it. The reality of doing may be opposed to thinking and speaking; that means 'perform(ing) on the stage of existence' (*The Oxford English Dictionary*, 1989, p.124).

If performance is an action or a multifaceted set of actions capable of influencing human attitudes and principles, architecture may also be an impressive combination of performances. According to Le Corbusier:

> We are here immersed in the full music of forms. Each one is there to play with those that surround it. Whether a palace or a house, each is governed by a similar intention; the intention ... of assimilating, of speaking clearly... Once we have drawn up the plan and the section, the game has started. There is the unity of the whole, the sculptural gamble, the temerity of the construction, the challenge. There are acrobatics, sport, and wit. We are enjoying ourselves; yes, we have had a wonderful time risking everything. (Le Corbusier, 1948, p.44)

According to the same author, the first thing to consider is to reduce shapes to the smallest size compatible with perfect functioning ('machine for living'). By enlarging the machine, we get the evolution of the form or the evolution of the actions-acts-activities.

Pictorial and architectural spaces: syntaxes of lines-codes

Space is inevitably related to everything concerning human life. Space, to vocabulary, has been related to time and duration as well, whereas space denoting area or extension is a linear distance or interval between two or more points or objects. An exceptionally interesting aspect of space can be found in the ancient Greek word *ch-òros*, which contains the root *òros* (meaning <u>edge</u>, boundary, but also rule). According to Le Corbusier, a form is the result of the right choice of a regulating diagram (geometry) of vertical and horizontal lines (rules). Diagrams are visible in any kind of contemporary art production, not only in architecture.

In his *Eye and Mind*, M. Merleau-Ponty says:

> My body simultaneously sees and is seen ... Visible and mobile, my body is thing among things; (form between other forms) ... But, because it moves itself and sees, it holds things in a circle around itself. (Merleau-Ponty, 1978, pp.58–59)

Also, Leonardo Da Vinci referred to the same primordial generating element of the pictorial image: the point. In excerpts of his *Treatise in Painting*, he affirmed:

> in the eye the shapes, the colours, all the images of the parts of the universe are reduced to a point and this point is such a marvellous thing ... In such a small space the image may be recreated by recomposing its expansion. (Kemp, et al, 1989, p.50)

Leonardo explains:

> The surface is the boundary ... and the boundary of a body is not part of that body, but the boundary of a body is the start of another. The boundaries of bodies are the least of all things. (Kemp, et al., 1989, p.53)

We can see clearly that Leonardo believes that forms are made of boundaries formed by lines and tensions between points. According to Walter Crane, historian, the mind must work through the eye; he also says:

> An eye trained to observe and select may, even in the dullest and dingiest street find artistic suggestions, if not in the buildings, then in the life. And where there is life, movement, humanity, there is sure to be character and interest. (Crane, 1904, p.151)

In *Logic and Design*, Krome Barratt, mathematician, affirms that emotions are aroused by symbols seen by the eye and by associated ideas (emotive fragments). Images can generate emotions and 'the intellect is the sum of all emotions' (Barratt, 1980, p.286). Forms and surfaces may offer emotional stimulation. The dramatisation of emotive fragments stimulates the intellect, the enrichment of forms and surfaces of the general environment 'acts as a social catalyst' (Barratt, 1980, p.286). 'A line is a path that can offer a pleasant and varied journey' (Barratt, 1980, p.186); having the opportunity to taste pleasant surprises, anybody wishes to repeat the same journey again and again. According to Krome Barratt, 'only the ever changing (line) is never changing'; lines are so powerful that they may be transformed from real life codes to eternal virtual reality regulating scales of artistic and architectural creativity.

Harmony dictated by universal natural laws can create a state of morality, if morality coincides with emotions. If equilibrium is so important in architecture, we can see why architects, like Le Corbusier or Natalini or Michelucci (figs 2 and 3) have been obsessed by geometry. Le Corbusier often spoke about n-dimension geometry in architecture; this meant that, by experimenting new geometry in architecture, he was playing down the whole morality of architecture itself. Performance is, anyway, something complex; it is not necessarily something literary and polemic.

Historically it has been proved that a moving point creates a line and this intentional movement in three dimensions can also fill a space. When a point moves along curved paths, then it is able to describe more complex areas and shapes, such as pictorial lines. There is always a meaningful purpose of the use of the line, such as that meaning its shared use in a society network or web. According to Krome Barratt, a path can be defined as 'a continuum of infinite length defining a finite space' (Barratt, 1980, p.170). Theories on the genesis of the built environment become extremely fascinating when we try to replace a point or points with real people; automatically abstraction of pictorial spaces could be transformed into a real urban environment by acquiring a complexity of systems based on lines and mathematics as a natural phenomenon of life.

According to Walter Crane, 'wave-lines' not only reveal movement, but also describe direction and force; that means wave-lines may represent human traffic flows into spaces. Organic flows of lines are interpenetrated images created by interweaving lines, which are present in maps as juxtaposed elements and, in specific territories or hidden paths, inside the built environment. We can find out that a line is highly performing when in contrast with another line or a group of lines and also that Sigmund Freud's assumption that people derive intense enjoyment only from a contrast and very little from a state of things, may be an obvious example.

One of the main components of performance is drama (action); drama is a communication of contrast, while anti-drama is a repetition that leads to apathy. Again, Krome Barratt insists that 'drama can be enriched beyond competition between two themes by the use of transitions and interweaving plots' (Barratt, 1980, p.301). It is obvious that rich dramas are required in every design and every design needs a scenario, which may be, for example, a town centre. By providing a scenario, 'a hierarchy

Fig.2. Giovanni Michelucci: a church project in San Miniato, Siena (1982) – This drawing belongs to the collection of the Giovanni Michelucci Foundation, Fiesole, Nr Florence. (Source: Belluzzi, A. & Conforti, C. (1987) <u>Lo Spazio Sacro di Michelucci – fotografie di Sgrilli, G.</u>, Siena : Umberto Allemandi & C. p.56)

Fig. 3. Giovanni Michelucci: project of the San Francesco a Guri church (1982) – This drawing belongs to the collection of the Giovanni Michelucci Foundation, Fiesole, Nr Florence. (Source: Belluzzi, A. & Conforti, C. (1987) <u>Lo Spazio Sacro di Michelucci – fotografie di Sgrilli, G.</u>, Siena : Umberto Allemandi & C. p.54)

of players and activities will emerge ... Any expectation is a projection into the future of past experiences or combination of those' (Barratt, 1980, p.301). The same kind of pathlines found in pictorial images can be also encountered in three-dimensional urban structures; urban genesis is a natural event which depends upon dynamic routes created by movement of highly active points-units (people's energy).

Important events can act as dynamic tensions or contrasts capable to set in movement cells' points into a cosmic ordered environment, such as that of a city. So, the codes adopted by most radical architects in the 1970s, like Adolfo Natalini, for example, have now evolved into paradigms following and preparing syntaxes for the future. All methods of communication with the wider societies taught by architects, like Giovanni Michelucci, have now been accepted by the latest generations of designers and architects; there is an unstoppable historical process still going on and heading towards the future.

I spent several years in research on Urbanism and had the opportunity to meet famous historians, experts in Urbanism, like Piero Sanpaolesi, urbanist and architectural historian, who strongly supported the idea of *interpenetrated images* and *interweaving* active lines inside the urban fabric of the city of Florence. In an unpublished study in 1975, Piero Sanpaolesi described his findings from research on a very important part of the centre of Florence in the north of the Cathedral: the area of the SS. Annunziata Church and the Convent in close proximity to the famous Innocenti Hospice. The whole area started developing in the thirteenth century and it is still considered as a district showing a high density of very important buildings with long history in arts and architecture. Today in the same district people unconsciously move along pathlines as preferential routes of human flows of traffic, as has always happened for many centuries since medieval times.

My research into pathlines in relation to the development of urban fabrics in cities and subsequent findings were reintroduced to the students I taught, particularly when they were trying to read and understand the built environment. In a sense history was repeating itself in learning and teaching in design and architecture. Radical ideas of the 1970s and perhaps from the whole previous century were easily transferred into today's student knowledge; the students' new experiences could now create real places for real people. I have selected a couple of images from the ideas development files (figs 4 and 5) of Rebecca Weldon, one of my students in 2005/06; in these images you can easily recognise the signs of teaching in her visual exploration of urban spaces and buildings.

Giovanni Michelucci declared towards the end of his life:

> No place has to change drastically; people's perceptions and prejudices must change ... a space is poor when it lacks human relationships and it is always beautiful when it encourages human encounters; there is always hope to explore such a space for many years to come. (Michelucci, 1993, pp.143–144)

Therefore, history goes on and on with teaching; history of architecture is simply the architects' eternal and ongoing history of learning, teaching and creating. I am really grateful to all my teachers as my academic career progress and my own teaching experience builds up at the same time. And I can also understand that perhaps the same will happen to my students one day; through my teaching they are able to capture and assimilate ideas and principles which will become *historical seeds* of transferable professional knowledge and formation. My teachers' teaching and the teaching of all generations before them has already passed into the high technological marvels of twenty-first century art, design and architecture and is going to prepare the everlasting performance act of lines for the future of the whole of humanity for years to come.

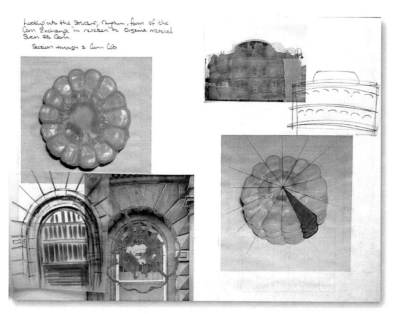

Fig. 4. Rebecca Weldon's student project: ideas development
(Interior Design, Leeds College of Art & Design, 2005–06)

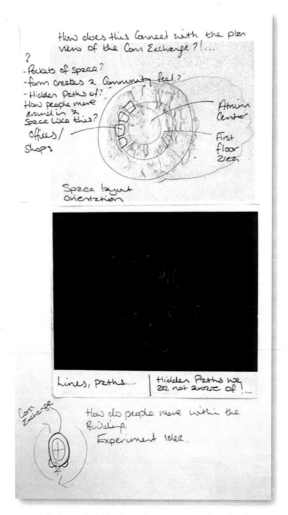

Fig. 5. Rebecca Weldon's student project: ideas development
(Interior Design, Leeds College of Art & Design, 2005–06)

Bibliography

Apollinaire, G. (1970) *The Cubist Painters* New York, G. Wittenburn publishers

Barratt, K. (1980) *Logic and Design: Art, Science and Mathematics* London, The Herbert Press

Branzi A. (1972) 'Il ruolo dell' avanguardia 2: L'Africa è vicina', *Casabella*, 364, p.2

Crane, W. (1904) *Line and Form* Manchester, George Bell and Sons

Ibelings, H. (2003) 'A Dutch Perspective on the Dutch architecture of Adolfo Natalini' in *Adolfo Natalini, Album Olandese* Florence, Aión Edizioni

Kemp, M. & Walker, M. (1989) *Leonardo on Painting* New Haven and London, Yale University Press

L'architecture d' aujourd'hui (1948) Special issue p.44

Manifesto 'IIa Mostra di Superarchitettura' (1967) Modena

Merleau-Ponty, M. (1978) 'Eye and Mind' in Osborne, H. (Ed.) *Aesthetics* Oxford, Oxford University Press

Michelucci, G. (1993) 'Un sogno, la capanna dell'angelo' in Bassi, G.B. (Ed.) *Alle Radici di Giovanni Michelucci: Pistoia come Luogo Felice* Firenze, Alinea editrice srl

Navone, P. & Orlandoni, B. (1974) *Architettura radicale* Segrate (Milan), G. Milani sas editrice

The Oxford English Dictionary, 2nd edition (1989) Oxford, Oxford University Press

Tracada, E. (1996) *Line performance act*, unpublished MA dissertation submitted in the Manchester Metropolitan University

Burslem School of Art, Queen Street Site, 12 July 2004.
Photographer Richard Smith © Permission Stoke-on-Trent College

A History of Design and Pedagogy at Burslem School of Art

Janine Sykes
Leeds College of Art and Design

Introduction

This paper is *timely*, as the subject is in honour of the (1907) centenary of the purpose-built Queen Street site of Burslem School of Art (BSA). The paper relates to the design history strand of the conference, by sharing some insights found in the writing of *Behind the Glass*, an article[1] honouring the unique achievements of the school. Commonalities with the latter and *Behind the Mosaic*, a publication honouring the (1903) centenary of the purpose built site at Vernon Street, at Leeds College of Art and Design, is apparent. Both studies focus in part on the contribution of the provincial schools to the national system, in terms of pedagogic design. This paper follows the growth and development of a practice-based pedagogy known as executed design, developed by a former student of BSA.

Transformation Design

The methodology for *Behind the Glass* and this paper is a mix of historical research, subjective knowledges,[2] and a contemporary approach known as transformation design (TD), practised by RED.[3] TD is user-centred and generated through the collaborative creativity of various groups in an organisation, including front-line workers, 'designers and managers together with consumers to improve the performance of organisations and deliver enhanced services' (Cottam et al., 2006, p.2). TD entails the belief that 'designers are uniquely placed to help solve complex social and economic problems' (Cottam et al., 2006 p.11) by implementing the design process to develop new solutions. As in *Behind the Glass*, TD functions to articulate a fascinating case study of pedagogic design and wider educational schemes, developed through a collaborative process which was totally student-centred.

---

1. Pending publication

2. The author worked in the creative studies department at Stoke-on-Trent College, Burslem 2001–2004 and is currently coordinator of contextual studies at LCAD.

3. A research body of the design council

In particular, it is found that as the former Principals of BSA were each prolific designers, they naturally applied design skills to educational structures.

Although the subject is essentially historical, the narrative twists intermittently to contemporary issues, as the boundaries of the learning environment extend once again to schools and the workplace. The scope of research for this paper includes *Art and the Beauty of the Earth* (1881), a lecture William Morris presented in Burslem, which provided a flavour of the ideals that influenced the school. Writings by two former Principals, Gordon Forsyth (1879–1952) and Reginald Haggar (1905–1988) were found to be invaluable. *A Centenary of Art Education in the Potteries* (1953) by Haggar gave a detailed account of the origins and growth of BSA from 1853, whereas *The Ideal School of Art* (1913), a speech by Forsyth, provided a vivid description of the school at the time. Writings by former student E.N. Scott (1904 & 1905) detailed the regional co-ordinated art education system developed by the former Principal Stanley Thorogood. Annie Eatwell (1989) provided a detailed chronology of Forsyth's training and career, which gave insights into the influences upon the educational methods he developed at BSA. An interview with former student (now artist) John Cooke proved to be useful in terms of giving details of the type of pedagogic approach practised at BSA in the post-war era. *Art Schools then and now* by Professor Rodgroff (2006) aids a critical discussion on contemporary art school pedagogy. Finally, the paper links to the recent research of Marie McLoughlin on Muriel Pemberton, 'Founder of St Martin's Fashion Course, and her role in the development of degree level fashion education in the UK … had first studied at Burslem School of Art' (McLoughlin, 2006, p.10). The selected research on those involved with BSA reveals the contribution BSA made to the history of design and pedagogy.

Contributions

Opened 10 October 1907, the purpose built site at Queen Street inherited a unique and progressive co-ordinated educational scheme that secured the foundations for the artistic talent that would walk its floors 'Clarice Cliff, Susie Cooper, William Moorcroft … Frederick Rhead … Muriel Pemberton …Terence Conran … Eduardo Paolozzi' (BSA, 1999). Founded in 1853,[4] BSA was the glasshouse that cultivated pioneering education practice; the type of design under the spotlight is pedagogic but understood in a holistic sense as part of a wider structure of a specialist-learning environment that reached beyond the art school walls into compulsory education and industry. The centenary year of the opening of the Queen Street site is the ideal opportunity to expose the contributions BSA made to design history and pedagogy. Like Boswell (2003) this paper asserts that these contributions by provincial schools deserve to be acknowledged.

> Quentin Bell, Stuart Macdonald and Christopher Frayling have unravelled how the Schools of Design were created … but there have been fewer attempts to trace these through provincial Schools and the climates of local artistic opinion. (Boswell, 2003, p17)

Unlike Leeds College of Art & Design (LCAD), BSA no longer exists. Like many provincial schools the institution was absorbed by the local FE (Stoke-on-Trent & Newcastle-under-Lyme) colleges and HE (Staffordshire University) provision, as a result of the 1988 reforms. It is interesting to ponder

---

4. BSA has a history of phases and expansions and like LCAD, BSA derived from art instruction in a Mechanics' Institute: The Potteries Mechanics' Institute established in 1830 in Fredrick St. Shelton – erected by public subscription' (Haggar, 1953, p10) From the Mechanics Institute, art classes progressed to rented premises in Burslem and eventually evolved into two subsequent architectural beauties: the Wedgwood Memorial Institute (1873) and the site at Queen Street (1907).

what the decline of the provincial art school means in the twenty-first century, as in the nineteenth century Morris believed that their presence reflected how art was valued: 'As far as our schools of art go … among all they have done not the least is that public recognition of the value of art in general which their very existence implies.' (Morris, 1881 in Smith 1962, p.26)

These words of William Morris[5] were spoken in Burslem where the invited speaker composed a substantial lecture titled *Art and The Beauty of the Earth*. Among the ideas presented was revolution, and Morris pointed to the provincial art school as the site and the pedagogic practice-executed design as the means. 'Those of you especially who are designing for goods, try to get the most out of your material … something should be done with it which is specially natural to it.' (Morris, 1881, p.28)

Executed design

Executed design essentially is a hands-on approach, which refers to working in the material for which the design was intended rather than on paper (Everitt, 2000) – clearly an Arts and Crafts pedagogy. The term was coined by the pioneering educationalist Edward Taylor (1838–1912), a former student of BSA who became Principal of Schools at Lincoln (1862) and Birmingham (1877–1903). Taylor was the first individual (through the provincial art school route) to confront centralised directives with this practice-led pedagogy. Inspired by his training at BSA, Taylor later implemented the model at Birmingham, which by the mid-twentieth century influenced the teaching of art and design nationally.

The 1946 report *Art Education* published by the Ministry of Education, praises the approach of training in the Midlands as being the most compatible to industry and advocated executed design as the national model, 'Through practical work in the material that the designer should be educated' (Ministry of Education, 1946, p.26). At this time a former student of LCAD, Percy H. Jowett (1882–1955) as Principal of the RCA (1935–47), secured executed design as the orthodox approach, and 'The ideas of the Art and Crafts Movement had been adopted and transformed into a new form of orthodox art education' (Boswell, 2003, p.31).

Progression

Overlapping these changes at the RCA, executed design continued at BSA through the then Principal Gordon Forsyth (1919–1944), a former student of Glasgow School of Art, the RCA[6] (1901–03) and Stoke Art School (1903). After his Art Directorship at Pilkington Tile and Pottery Company, Forsyth became Superintendent of Art Instruction for the five schools[7] of art in Stoke-on-Trent. At the outset of his new post, Forsyth inherited a progressive co-ordinated system of art education designed by the former Principal, Stanley Thorogood A.R.C.A. BSA was already the nucleus of a co-ordinated system of art education spanning a regional provision from primary to advanced levels, ensuring a seamless progression, 'with no misdirection or duplication' (Scott, 1904). This progressive scheme was documented by a former student, E.N.Scott (1904), and it is clear from Scott's descriptions that executed design was implemented in the workshops at BSA: 'every faculty is provided by the education

5. This speech was printed by Chiswick Press in 1898 in golden type, designed by Morris for the Kelmscott Press. Published by Longmans & Co.

6. Tutors included William Lethaby, Christopher Whall (stained glass) and Edward Johnson (calligraphy).

7. Tunstall, Burslem, Stoke, Longton and Hanley

authority, with the co-operation of the manufacturers, for the execution of designs in the material for which they are intended' (Scott, 1904, p.135). Also, as each faculty had the co-operation of the wider community, the educational structure could be considered an early form of TD.

Scott (1904) details how Thorogood's series of standards and objectives were outlined from I to VII, from memory drawing to pattern formation. Gradations began from elementary school to evening classes and beyond to full time specialist study. Scott evidences that the Thorogood system was pioneering by pointing to the collection of medals won at international exhibitions and commendations from art inspectors. This pioneering system was designed to promote progression, which is also an objective of the National Arts Learning Network (NALN) today, where 'more learners with vocational qualifications or at work progress to selective specialist programmes in art, design and the performing arts' (Bichard, 2006).

Forsyth

On 10 October 1907 *The Staffordshire Sentinel* read, 'The New School of Art at Burslem, To-Day's Opening Ceremony'. The article is a glossary profiling those responsible for the new school, from the architect to the mayor who donated the land. Twelve years later Forsyth became Superintendent of Art Instruction and, like Thorogood, was based at Queen Street, where he taught painting and graphics. However, prior to this appointment and the interruptions of the war, Forsyth gave a lecture at Stoke Town Hall, titled *An Ideal School of Art;* which gives us an insight into Forsyth's Republic, much of which he built six years later. For Forsyth, the purpose of an art school was to cultivate the inner self and, in contrast to the development of scientific subjects, was an immeasurable feat. Forsyth praises BSA as an ideal, particularly in terms of the pedagogy, which was based on a craftsman learning a trade, and was 'a model in equipment and arrangement, and pre-eminently a place to work in and not for ornament' (Forsyth, 1913). Forsyth also outlined a co-ordinated approach to art training, on similar lines to Thorogood's, where the curricular began in school where children were first trained in methods of perspective and memory. Also, like Thorogood's, the main objectives were the command over materials; in drawing, pencil and brush, in painting pure colour. Once line and colour were mastered, personal explorations were reviewed with guidance from a workshop master. This explorative aspect of materials and a preference for tacit knowledge can be seen to link with the paper by Samantha Broadhead, which traces the pedagogical models followed by LCAD in the development of the post-war basic design course that in turn informed the foundation diploma course we know today.

Returning to Forsyth's speech, the ideal tutors should be made from local material, as they would understand both the students and regional industries better. Another significant point he made was that at advanced levels, the best rewards for learners would be the opportunity to undertake live briefs, 'by far the best prize that could be given to a student was work – actual work to do' (Forsyth, 1913). Again, it is interesting to note that these values still continue today in the National Diploma courses and Foundation Degrees, where work-based training is highly valued and employers are involved in 'work-based modules, provision of work experience placements, and assessment of student performance' (HEFCE, 2000 p.8). Forsyth also underlined the function of the provincial schools, which interestingly has many affinities with the Bauhaus manifesto: 'Let the architects design beautiful buildings for the municipality, the modellers do the sculpture, the painters decorate the walls, and their craftsmen also help to beautify it' (Forsyth, 1913).

Burslem and Weimar

Between Forsyth's prophesising speech and the superintendence post at BSA came the war. Forsyth shared the same generation and objectives as Gropius, and for each the war was an event that provided a vantage point for reflection and an insatiable appetite for reforming the design industries. This clear-sightedness and readiness for change is evident in a letter Forsyth wrote in 1918 to the editor of the *Staffordshire Sentinel*:

> With a little bit of the fighting spirit not wholly died down and perhaps a little bit fresher point of view than those who have been in more immediate touch with the industry. (Forsyth, 1918)

In 1919 both Gropius and Forsyth assumed their strategic positions, Gropius Director of the Bauhaus in Wiemar and Forsyth Superintendent of Art in Stoke-on-Trent. Both institutions were established in ideal locations for their respective disciplines and industries. Like Gropius, Forsyth looked to art education as a route to building a new future, while being critical of the industrialists who failed to invest in design education throughout the war years: 'enemy countries were making giant strides in competitive markets through the very same characteristics as we were blindly refusing to accept' (Forsyth, 1918, p.3).

Overall, Eatwell (1989) asserts that Forsyth's great contribution was the continuation of the 'creative craftsmanship model, an approach compatible with industry', an approach not dissimilar to that implemented in Weimar. At Burslem, this craft-based approach permeated from 'hand painting' in the school workshops to the factory studio through a generation of students such as Susie Cooper and Clarice Cliff. Thereby the pedagogy practised at BSA influenced the processes in industry.

Another former principal of BSA, Reginald Haggar (1905–1988) believed Forsyth's most significant contribution was as a painter with the development of a brush-drawn technique, a method that he passed to his students. As evidence of Forsyth's standard of watercolour work, Haggar (1953) pointed to Forsyth's interior of York Minster (1927), now housed at Leeds City Art Gallery. It is argued here however, that Forsyth's greatest contribution was his application of the design process to art education at BSA.

In recognition of his achievements, Forsyth was appointed as Art Advisor to the British Manufacturers Federation in 1921 and 'it was Forsyth who reviewed the British contribution to the International Exhibition at Paris in 1925 (Eatwell, 1989, p 28). Also in 1925, BSA was inspected and staff were found to be working in the craft disciplines they taught and a Junior Art Course commenced for learners aged 13 to 15 years. The Junior Course was to become a great success, giving school leavers the skills to walk into employment or the opportunity to progress to part-time or full-time courses. Again, colliding with a contemporary aim of NALN, 'The key aim of the NALN is to increase the number of learners progressing from vocational programmes, or the workplace into higher education' (NALN, 2005).

Throughout his superintendence, Forsyth clearly applied design solutions to the administration and co-ordination of BSA, the ability to extend the application of design happens to be a main trait of TD. Similarly, the recent pilots of specialist diplomas in the creative arts currently implemented in schools offer clear progression routes to FE and HE, which again echo the Thorogood scheme. Executed design continued at Burslem after Forsyth stepped down from his superintendence, as was evident through an interview and writings of former student John Cooke:

As a student the lecturers used to talk about 'the integrity of the medium'… the medium be it paint, clay, charcoal, has an inherent beauty of its own and it is up to the artist … to retain this beauty rather than let it become smothered in the struggle to represent the subject (Cooke, 2005, p.26)

Cooke was part of the first cohort of the National Diploma in Design (NDD), which the aforementioned (1946) post-war government report had outlined and recommended the pedagogy practised in the Midlands. According to Frith and Horn (1987) the pedagogy practised in the art schools of the post-war period was known as the 'civilizing ideal', where students were actively involved in the construction of the curricula, and it was this quality that defined art schools from the rest of higher education. Interestingly, TD entails involving the ideas of the user or consumer with the design of a service.

Rogoff (2006) highlights the bureaucracy and result-orientated culture present in British higher education today as being in a discordance with contemporary art school pedagogy, where process and investigation is paramount. Rogoff explains that this unruly pedagogy is problematic due to its unpredictable nature:

Odd, then that such an unstable pedagogy should have been captured and held hostage by such an overwhelming bureaucracy – unless perhaps the bureaucracy is afraid of the very challenge such an approach would represent to its sovereignty. (Rogoff, 2006 p.7)

Rogoff offers a solution to educationists: 'we need to learn to live in parallel rather than in conflicted economies: moving sideways … engaging in numerous non-legitimated processes' (Rogoff, 2006, p.147). Perhaps the application of design solutions is the key to resolving issues within an increasingly complex bureaucracy, just as Forsyth found in his day.

Although the evangelical language of Morris and Forsyth seems outmoded today, the conviction that investment in a specialist art and design education is necessary for the well-being of both society and industry is an interesting notion to return to, particularly as 'The creative industries are becoming ever more significant in the UK, and represent a larger proportion of the economy than anywhere else in the world.' Bichard, 2005, p.3). Also, the findings from a recent report by UNICEF that assessed the well being of young people across the economically advanced nations found that 30% of adolescents aged 15–19 years in the UK expect to find low-skilled work. Other high rates were found in low self-esteem and dissatisfaction. The appearance of specialist diplomas and foundation degrees in the early twenty-first century perhaps signifies the return of a need for a skilled and satisfied workforce.

This brief genealogy of BSA included a narrative of a pedagogy that grew from the grass roots of provincial schools and the design industries in the Midlands. Executed design was part of a wider arts and crafts approach that placed value on 'the vernacular' – interestingly an aspect celebrated in postmodernity.

This paper has consistently confused design history with contemporary educational practice, in order to bring attention to certain traits found in both TD and the design processes applied by Thorogood and Forsyth to enhance the art education of Stoke-on-Trent. Further details of how the holistic design of BSA, including the architecture, is an early example of TD, are revealed in *Behind the Glass*, thereby, bringing the newness of this type of design into question. Examples of co-ordination, progression and transformation design have all been shown to exist in the annals of design history and pedagogy.

Bibliography

Bichard, M. (September 2005) National Arts Learning Network (NALN) *A HEFCE- funded lifelong learning network* <www.arts.ac.uk/docs/NALN1.pdf > (23/09/2006)

Broadhead, S. (2007) *Tensions Between the Construction of Design Knowledge in Art Colleges and in Schools* Paper, Design and Pedagogy Conference 16 March 2007 Leeds, Leeds College of Art and Design

Burslem School of Art *Information Pack* (1999)

Cooke, J. (2005) *As I See IT* Jackdaw March No. 46, p.26, London

Cooke, J. (26 July 2006) Telephone Interview

Cottam, H. Burns, C. Vanstone, C. Winhall, J. (2006) 'Transformation Design' *RED Paper 02,* 6 February <http://www.designcouncil.info/mt/RED/transformationdesign/> (11/06/2006)

Eatwell, A. (1989) 'Gordon Mitchell Forsyth (1879–1952) – Artist, Designer and Father of Art Education in the Potteries' *Journal of Decorative Arts Society* Vol. 13, pp.27–32

Evening Sentinel (1952) *Industry's Dept to Mr. Gordon Forsyth: Distinguished Artist And Ceramic Expert* 22 December p.4 Stoke-On-Trent, Sentinel Newspapers Ltd

Everitt, S. (2000) *Birmingham Institute of Art and Design* <http://www.biad.uce.ac.uk/archives/> (03/06/2006)

Forsyth, G. M. (1918) *Future of Pottery Industry. Mr Gordon Forsyth on the Need for Better Design (to the Editor of the 'Sentinel')* The Staffordshire Sentinel 3 December p.3, Stoke-On-Trent, Sentinel Newspapers Ltd

Frith, S. & Horne, H. (1987) *Art into Pop* London, Methuen Young Books

Haggar, R.G. R.I., A.R.C.A, F.R.S.A (1953) *A Centenary Of Art Education In The Potteries, with notes on the artists*

Haggar, R. G. R.I., A.R.C.A, F.R.S.A (1954) 'Gordon Mitchell Forsyth R. I., A.R.C.A.' in *Staffordshire Life,* Spring pp.20, 21 & 27

HEFCE (2000) *Foundation degree prospectus* <http://www.hefce.ac.uk/Pubs/hefce/2000/00_27.pdf > (3/01/2007)

Mackail, J.W. (1899) *Life of William Morris* in SMITH, H.P (Ed) (1962) *William Morris, Art and the beauty of the earth, a lecture delivered at Burslem Town Hall Oct 13th 1881* Adult and Education Society Series, Documentary No. 7, Oxford Published from 27 Harley Rd, Oxford

McLoughin, M. (2006) *The Wedgwood Institute, Burslem; and its contribution to English Design* (Conference abstract pp.10–11) Gladstone Centre for Victorian Studies, St Deinio's Library *Citizenship, Identity and Nation in the Long Nineteenth- Century,* Manchester, University of Manchester

Miller, C. (Ed) (2003) *Behind the Mosaic; One Hundred Years of Art Education* Leeds Museums and Galleries in collaboration with Leeds College of Art and Design Sheffield, J. W. Northend

MOE Ministry of Education (1946) *Art Education* Pamphlet No. 6 London, HMSO

Rogoff, I. (2006) 'Art Schools then and now' *Frieze, Contemporary Art and Culture* September Issue, No. 101 pp.142–147

Scott, E. N. (1904) 'Co-ordinated Art Education At Burslem' *The Studio,* (Vol. No.32) pp.132–136

Scott, E. N. (1905) 'The Ceramic Work Of The Burslem Art School' *The Studio* Vol. 36 No.151 October pp.333–340

Smith, H. P. (Ed) (1962) *William Morris, Art and the Beauty of the Earth, A Lecture delivered at Burslem Town Hall, October 13th 1881* Adult Education and Society Series, Documentary No. 7, Oxford

The Staffordshire Sentinel (1913) 'Mr. Forsyth' s Lecture. Mr. Gordon M. Forsyth. A.R.C.A. The Art School and The Craft of the Potter' 18 September Stoke-On-Trent, Sentinel Newspapers Ltd

The Staffordshire Sentinel (1907) 'The New School of Art at Burslem. Today's Opening Ceremony' 10 October pp.3–14: Stoke-On-Trent, Sentinel Newspapers Ltd

The Construction of Design Knowledge in Art Colleges and Schools:
A Case Study of the GCSE Applied Art and Design

Samantha Broadhead
Leeds College of Art and Design

Context

Leeds College of Art and Design has run an Applied Art and Design GCSE for the last three years at the Vernon Street Campus. It was created for 14–16 year-old students who for the majority of the week studied in school, but also came into college for one day. The original aims of the course were to introduce school pupils to the experience of studying art in a college and for them to make use of the specialist resources (ceramics room, photography darkroom and printmaking workshop). The local schools selected those who had demonstrated an interest in art and design and may not have been achieving their potential in a school environment.

This paper is a discussion about the possible tensions that school pupils may have experienced when studying at school and art college concurrently. Although there may have been many cultural differences between the school and college learning environment, the debate will focus on the differences of how knowledge was constructed in school and in college. The main argument is that art and design knowledge was delivered to students in schools in such a way that often focused on practicing drawing and painting skills and the imitation of canonical styles (Addison, 1999 in Hardy, 2006, p.115). This was seen when the college staff interviewed the pupils selected for the course. The work that students brought with them was often reproductions of images by well-known artists, the implication being that students were learning about what already had been discovered or experienced by others and were reproducing predestined ways of doing things. In colleges the students are expected to find out for themselves about design and in some ways construct their own art and design knowledge. This is done through experiential learning and self-evaluation.

Firstly, it will be argued that tutors from Leeds College of Art and Design, working on the GCSE and other programmes, historically use a particular pedagogical model that is partly derived from the Bauhaus principles and the notion of executed design. Evidence for this can be found in the historical records from the college archive from the 1950s onwards when the College was under the leadership of Eric Taylor (1956–1970). These ideas continue to be important in contemporary art and design education (Robins in Addison and Burgess, 2003). Writers, teachers and practitioners from the 1950s and 1960s like Eric Taylor, Alan Davie and Roger Coleman have remained important as they were

Year One	2D Visual Studies	3D Visual Studies	Printmaking
Year Two	Visual Studies	Project Research	Project Development

Fig. 1. Applied GCSE Art and Design Structure based on students from schools attending art college one day a week

First six Months Preliminary Course (Vorkurs)	Elementary study of form		
3 Years Integration of art and craft	Space, colour, composition, Study		Study of Materials
	Colour	Textiles	Metal
Site Testing and Design, Building and Engineering Science			

Fig. 2. Diagram derived from the Bauhaus curriculum 1922

concerned with issues about art and design education which are relevant today. Of particular concern was the relationship of art and design in secondary education to what happened in art colleges. Such historical sources also provided a link to earlier Bauhaus models and philosophies of education. When comparing the organisation and delivery of the GCSE in Applied Art and Design, 2008 (fig. 1) with that of the original 1922 Bauhaus curriculum (fig. 2) it could be seen that both shared a similar structure. The idea of a period of time (in the Applied GCSE course it was one year part-time, the Bauhaus six months full-time), where a student could explore visual language and a range of workshops, remained central to a general art and design course within the Art College. Other evidence comes from the tutor's own learning biographies where they themselves studied under the Foundation Course model of art and design education where these design pedagogical philosophies have been practised.

Textiles	Photography	Ceramics	I.T.	Looking at other artists, designers and craftspeople
Visualisation		Project Presentation		Project Evaluation

Study of Materials in the Basic workshops			
Study of Nature	Study of materials and Tools	Study of Construction and representation	
Wood	Stone	Clay	Glass

Secondly, it will be argued that the art college model was very different from the student's usual experience of learning. The notion of *school knowledge* will be explored using a definition used by Donald Schon (1987). The hegemony of school knowledge can be seen in the ways that schools delivered art and design. This formed the basis of Swift and Steers' critique of art and design education in schools (1999 in Addison, 2006, pp.17–25). The reasons why this way of education was so dominant will be discussed by using Diana Cheng-Man Lau's concept of the modern curriculum (2001).

Thirdly, the possible tensions resulting from the exposure of the GCSE Applied Art and Design students to two different philosophies of learning will be investigated. The ways in which these tensions can influence behaviour and learning identities will be explored along with the notions of turning points and transitions.

Historical Debates

I will explore the process of these developments further in terms of their historical progression, featuring key theorists and practitioners who have contributed to the debate. Stuart Boyd Davis (2000) wrote in *Educating the Multimedia Designer* that art schools have,

> …distinctive traditions such as individual experimentation, a close contact with materials and technologies and an encouragement to explore the limits of the subject. (Boyd Davis in Dudley and Mealing, 2000 p.64)

It could be argued that Leeds College of Art and Design shared in this distinctiveness, with a pedagogical history rich in student centered learning. Indeed, the original Leeds College of Art used this method of delivery in the *Basic Design Course,* which was the basis of what is now know as the Foundation Course. At least there was some influence from the Bauhaus. Evidence for this can be seen in a document found in the college archives called *The Developing Process: Work in Progress Towards a New Foundation of Art Teaching* developed at the department of Fine Art, Kings College, Durham University and at Leeds College of Art, published in 1959 (fig. 3 and 3a). This document explains and expands the philosophy of art and design education dominant in the college and in particular the Foundation Course in Art and Design.

> As a concept of Art education, basic design has its origins in the Bauhaus particularly in the pedagogic work of Klee and Kandinsky and the teaching programme of Johannes Itten. (Coleman, 1959, p.1)

This could be seen as a student's own exploration of the formal elements of design such as line, form, colour and space. The tutor set certain exercises where the student could discover for themselves through experimentation the characteristics of this visual and tacit knowledge. One key feature of the philosophy at Leeds College of Art in the 1950s was that it sought to eradicate the boundaries between fine art and applied art and that there was a common language that is the basis of both art and design disciplines. Even now in its current programmes, such as Access to Art and Design and the Foundation Course, design students and fine art students are taught together for the initial stages of their course.

> From the middle of the nineteenth century to the foundation of the Bauhaus the most progressive attempts to reform art education have resolved around the bringing together of fine and applied art. (Coleman, 1959, p.1)

There was also a notion that art and design should include other subjects such as mathematics and general studies. Again there was a wish to make connections between various areas of knowledge, rather than keeping them separate. Eric Taylor put this forward in later writings when he said,

> It has been that General Studies fail when considered as something separate – an extra subject added to its syllabus and succeed when associated with student's own ideas … not only a broadening but deepening effect. (Taylor, 1967, p.2)

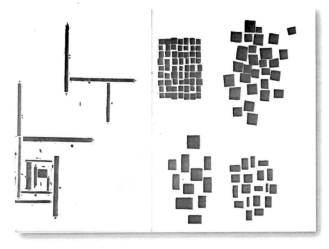

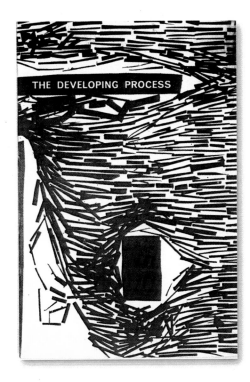 is inside the first crop showing the book cover "THE DEVELOPING PROCESS".

Fig. 3. The Developing Process: *Work in Progress Towards a New Foundation of Art Teaching (1959)* a programme developed by Durham University and Leeds College of Art

Fig. 3a. Pages 9–10, examples of student experimentation in line and shape

Taylor lamented in an article written for *The Yorkshire Post* (1971) called 'The Artist in a Machine Age' the choices young people had to make within school where the sciences and the arts were separated. He feels that this way of ordering and classifying knowledge was not in the student's interests. Implicit in this was that the interconnectedness of knowledge rather than increased specialisation at a young age was what was important.

> Most of us have seen through personal experience or that of our children the agencies of the decision made at the age of 12–14 regarding whether to tread the path of science or the arts, and how difficult it is now to find the student entering further education who has an understanding of both … the common language of the nautilus shell, interdisciplinary mathematics, sciences … (Taylor, 1971)

But mostly there was the idea that the students discover knowledge for themselves. The emphasis is on an individual's creative journey. Alan Davie, who was a Gregory Fellow from Leeds University in the 1950s, explained this. He wrote in detail about how he taught drawing and in doing so described a model of experiential learning.

> It is difficult to rid oneself of false concepts of art based upon knowledge and cleverness, and no teacher-student relationship can be satisfactory if it is one between a superior (knowing) and an inferior (ignorant). One must learn to have faith in intuition that 'knows' without knowledge. (Davie, 1959, p.27)

Within this piece of writing Davie seemed to be arguing for a more equal relationship between tutor and student where both have the potential to be *knowing*. He used words like 'faith' and 'intuition'. It was as if the tutor must have faith that the student would discover something of value, perhaps not intervene or control the learning process too much. The tutor was not the holder of knowledge but in some ways may have had more experience.

> To demonstrate the dynamic of the creative force I usually begin with simple exercises in pure idealess activity: direct putting down of black marks, with no end in view, purposeless and aimless. Strangely enough the student finds that to work without thought requires a great deal of mental discipline and it is some time before he can achieve an image without the intermediary of reasoning. (Davie, 1959, p.27)

Here, the characteristics of the materials were explored without the tutor saying what the correct way of using the charcoal was. Rather than imitating though copying another artist's style or mimicking a skill learnt though watching a demonstration, the student was finding his or her own way of mark-making. By working with no end in view that action of mark-making could be considered almost with a sense of *being in the moment*. When this activity was done with school students they founnd it difficult to work without an end in view, often wanting to illustrate rather than make marks.

> The next stage entails the introduction of idea but idea must also be intuitive without preliminary discrimination or attachment. I always encourage the use of irrational or crazy ideas, and the result of intuitive action will always be distinct and positive. Woolly work comes from woolly thinking. Dynamic results are obtained when students are urged to try for bad or illogical placings; the outcome of proper exploration of the unknown. (Davie, 1959, p.27)

This was interesting because Davie encouraged breaking any rules the student may have previously learned. He tried to get students to get rid of preliminary discrimination or attachment by trying compositions that are bad and illogical. It was as if trying to imagine the outcome before the action has been performed was a device that restricted creativity. It was only when students were prepared to try the unexpected that new design knowledge could be created. This was generated through the process. The tutor facilitated the process rather than decided exactly what was to be learned.

> Having achieved, after a massive pile of work, through various exercises on many mediums a faith in the magical inner creative force, the student can now enter his chosen field of creativity, confident in his new formed freedom which embraces the known with the unknowable, logical with the magical life can have a oneness which is both real and unreal. (Davie, 1959, p.27)

This final statement revealed the extent to which the tutor was not in control of the final outcomes of the learning experience. Words like magical and unknowable hinted at the belief that the learning process is partly hidden from the tutor. These ideas are set within the historical context of the 1950s but they still informed decisions about the organisation and delivery of art and design today. When looking at fig. 1 it can be seen that the applied GCSE has been organised along the ideas of the Bauhaus (fig. 2). The first year was dedicated to experiential learning in the workshops (ceramics, photography, printmaking and multi-media) and also in visual language. Running concurrently was the use of self-evaluation as an opportunity for students to reflect on their experiences. The delivery focus here was on experimentation in a wide range of media using a range of visual language. The second year of the course was the application of the students' previous experiences to an art and design project set by the awarding body. The delivery of this stage was more personalised; a whole term was given over to students' risk-taking with ideas, materials and visual language before any attempt to answer the brief was made. Individual learning plans recorded objectives that were specific to the individual student, decided through discussion with the tutor. Clearly, here the student's own input was important and to some extent the tutor was facilitating the process rather than deciding exactly what the student should be learning. There was therefore an opportunity for Davie's original ideas about trying the unexpected to be encouraged in a contemporary context.

Schools and Art Colleges: Comparing Pedagogical Structures

It could be argued when looking at Leeds College of Art and Design staff's own educational experience that they have followed the Foundation model of education (Foundation diplomas were achieved by staff at Batley college of Art, Wakefield College, Leeds College of Art and Design and Scarborough College of Art). Effectively, tutors often model their own teachers in their teaching practice (Goodlad 1990; Britzman, 1991; Lortie, 1975). So while working within an art and design institution that has a long history of student centered and experiential learning, the school pupils were exposed to staff who had also been through that same process. But were the educational experiences of teachers in schools so very different from their colleagues within colleges? The Department of Education and Science said that in 1983 most art and design teachers had qualifications from art colleges and postgraduate certificates in teacher training (DfES, 1983, p.62). College tutors were more likely to have done teacher training in post- compulsory rather than secondary education. Robins has said that secondary teachers may not have agreed with the teaching philosophy they employed to get high grades but did not want to risk failure; their own values learnt on foundation courses meant they did not necessarily agree with what they are teaching. They persisted in teaching because of the pressure of external testing (Robins in Addison and Burgess, 2003, p. 43).

School pupils may have been coming into college to study because they were attracted to the differences between the ways art and design was taught there compared with school. The most basic reason for this could be the structure of the school timetable. Pupils currently have their school day split up into different subjects that are delivered in different classrooms. The amount of time an art and design class may be only as little as one hour. As a result, design knowledge in schools was separated from other forms of knowledge and the relationships between art and other subjects like science which were valued by educators like Taylor (1971), were diminished. Within college there was the luxury of a whole day given over to art and design investigation and evaluation.

> Art schools are full of artists, they are dominated by students who have done art at school and who, thanks to the restrictive tendencies of school timetabling, were encouraged to drop science and technological subjects. (Boyd Davis in Dudley and Mealing, 2000 p.66)

Other timetabling strategies such as rotating art and design with other subjects could also lessen the time and fragment the continuity of delivery in the first three years of secondary school (DfSE, 1983, p.62). Factors like the access to resources, storage and space along with class sizes also affected the breadth of what is covered in an art and design programme (DfSE, 1983, p.61–62). Such organisational matters may in part explain the reasons why art and design knowledge was constructed and delivered differently in schools. I would argue that the dominant content in art and design in schools was painting and drawing and the copying of canonical styles. This was seen when college staff interviewed school students before they started the course, as their sketchbooks were filled with copies from popular culture and larger works often were copies of early twentiethcentury art. Addison said that this is the centre of primary and secondary education where students learn to copy and transcribe. He had some critical points about this mode of art and design education:

> At secondary level, with its analytical imperatives and tools, the process of transcription focuses on the more superficial task of the imitation of the surface. This is not without its benefits, but it is a time-consuming task that offers no understanding of either the process of making (the pupil imitates the outcome, usually the photographic reproduction, not the practice of transforming perceptions/conceptions into sensible form) nor any historical or contextual investigation. (Addison, 1999 in Hardy, 2006 p.116)

This may exemplify the possible narrowing and control of the art and design knowledge that students were exposed to, firstly by concentrating on canonical early European modernist works. Secondly, the students were copying stylistic conventions already conceived by someone else, and therefore the experimental and experiential underpinnings of modernist art and design were lost, becoming style without content. Thirdly, this approach was safe territory for both tutors and students; by copying images and styles that have stood the test of time there was less opportunity to take risks and consider the unexpected. In this sense, students may not have engaged with the processes of creativity or experienced materials. Swift and Steers (1999 in Hardy, 2006) in their *Manifesto for Art in Schools* appeared to confirm this analysis of school art and design education. Amongst several other issues they identified teaching that used limited and orthodox approaches to art and design that gave students limited media and learning opportunities and encouraged outcome or product-led work. Students, they argued, had insufficient autonomy and lack of choice. In order to change the status quo in schools, they stated that,

> Teachers should be helped to enjoy the means of discovery and risk-taking inherent in experimental practice and thought. (Swift and Steers, 1999 in Hardy, 2006, pp.20–12)

Interestingly, Swift and Steers offered the idea that the teacher should also be a participating discoverer and learner. The ideas they were describing were similar to those Davie was recommending back in the late 1950s and which have remained with the pedagogical practices of the Art and Design College. The call for increased student autonomy and a re-examination of the relationship between tutors and students has been made for crafts taught at HE level. Ball, (1996) talked about the value of students taking responsibility for their own learning by setting own goals and self-evaluation. Tutors were seen as 'role models, as professionals and independent learners in their own right' (Ball, 1996, pp.121–124). This approach, where students could construct their own art and design knowledge through experience and reflection, could be used throughout all stages of education.

Summary of Schon's Argument

At this point the notion of school knowledge should be discussed. This was a concept described by Donald Schon in *Educating the Reflective Practitioner*, a paper given to the 1987 meeting of the American Educational Research Association, Washington DC. Educational philosophers such as Rousseau and Dewey informed Schon's ideas. He sought to encourage tutors to be responsive to students' learning by using reflective practices. It could be argued that Schon was talking about a similar educational process to the one Alan Davie was describing in the 1950s.

Schon argued that school knowledge is the dominant epistemology of the school institution. He described it as being about control and predictability because these are features of all bureaucracies. Here the tension between Davies' ideas about the uncertainty of the unknowable and the definite school knowledge becomes evident. To summarise Schon's ideas, he said that school knowledge saw what we know as a product and 'It's the business of the teachers to know what the right answers are and to communicate them to students.' (1987). Schon suggested that knowledge was valued the more theoretical it was. Knowledge was also seen as modular and as something that could be built up into more complex patterns of understanding.

This approach to teaching art and design as a form of school knowledge, in particular, left little room for students to take risks, experiment and explore new ideas, to construct their own design knowledge. This view of knowledge as a body or end in itself was in opposition to art school educational values. Merete Bates in 1968 summarised Harry Thubron's (leader of the Basic Design Course) attitude in 1950s as being 'the process of education is more important than the result, the most important of all is a creative attitude to life' (Bates, 1968). Knowledge as a fixed end product was of secondary importance to the process of learning that could be used throughout a student's learning career.

As to why this way of teaching school knowledge has been prevalent in schools was explained in a paper by Diana Cheng-Man Lau, (2001, p.34) *Analysing Curriculum Development Process: Three Models*. She proposed that the modern model of education appeared rational, logical and was controlled by outside drivers rather than students and teachers. Therefore, the students had a passive role in the education process within schools (Thorpe, 1993), where they received knowledge rather than actively discovered it. This appeared to reflect the management model which education sometimes emulated. So, applying this to art and design within schools, what constitutes design knowledge was decided outside the classroom, delivered by teachers and received by students. Within the classroom school students remain in a very subordinate position, 'where challenges to the learning agenda were not expected …' (Wyatt-Smith and Cumming, 2003, p.52). When looking at other school subjects like English, knowledge was seen as 'ready made' (Wilson, 2001 in Wyatt-Smith and Cumming, 2003, p.52), to be received by students and then represented back through assessment rather than constructed or developed. This is in contrast to the art school learning experience where, 'We try to teach them how to think round corners, how to make creative jumps – not how to follow cause and effect' (Taylor in Bates, 1968). Design knowledge could be discovered without always being rational and methodical.

Schon further described how using a form of learning that is based on problem solving in a workshop or studio (he used the example of an architecture design studio) could cause feelings of confusion, vulnerability and even hostility in the students. They may have felt they did not know what they were doing, losing confidence, and feeling incompetent (Schon, 1987).

However, even though this is the case, he writes:

> I believe, the experience of the students in any reflective practicum is that they must plunge into the doing, and try to educate themselves before they know what it is they're trying to learn. *The teachers cannot tell them.* (Schon, 1987)

Schon made the point that this way of learning could evoke, initially, quite negative emotions that could even turn to anger and in this sense has described tensions students could experience. When exposing a group of school students who were familiar with 'school knowledge' to an art school environment where the dominant mode of delivery involved experimentation, exploration and problem-solving where the tutors 'set the scene but do not direct the play' (Thompson, 1985, in Miller, 2003, p.63), the emotions these students felt became apparent. When considering the GCSE Applied Art and Design group, individuals have demonstrated anger and frustration through disruptive behaviour or screwing their own work up and throwing it away. Students' behaviour within the college could indicate that they were more used to receiving school knowledge from the tutor rather than experimenting for themselves. Examples of this behaviour could be making marks that are illustrative rather than explorative, a reluctance to make choices without a tutor's reassurance and copying others in class. All these examples of behaviour perhaps indicate a lack of confidence in the student's own capacity to make creative decisions which would improve with more experience. Along with differences in teaching approaches, when entering the college system, school students also experienced a new structure to their day where they spend more time working at art and design, so there was time to explore basic visual language and materials. Studying art and design in a new context could begin to feel uncomfortable or difficult for the student, a shock if they had always felt they excelled in this at school.

The GCSE teaching team encouraged the school students to take on the new ways of the art college mode of education, and to see themselves as art and design students. By working in a community of practice the student's identities could change. This related to the notion of 'turning points' put forward by Hodkinson, Sparkes and Hodkinson where over a short or extended duration of time a person goes through a transformation of identity and, in particular, young people begin to make 'significant, pragmatically rational career decisions' (1996, p.142). The hope was that the school pupils would see themselves as being part of the Art and Design College and feel happy to progress on full-time courses after the age of 16. For this to happen their experiences needed to be productive and purposeful.

However, it could be argued that there were some barriers to this. Some students could have felt comfortable with the school mode of learning and felt a lack of confidence in the college environment. They were also not fully submerged into the college timetable, being aware that they were in fact visitors, part-time art and design students at best. So while they created a new and distinctive learning identity for themselves, these identities could be about being 'alien' or 'other' to the Art and Design College environment. There were also contributing discourses of race, gender and in particular class that influenced this possible new identity. Could students from diverse backgrounds identify with other students within the college? Was the individual's own art and design knowledge that they brought with them to the college, constructed at home and at school, truly valued by the college tutors? A different approach to delivering art and design runs the risk of switching young people off from the subject and the institution.

Robins has talked about the transition from secondary to tertiary education, seeing the foundation course as a purge of school knowledge from the minds of A level students. She conceptualised secondary students as the 'great unwashed' who needed to be cleansed by immersion into art school pedagogical practices. She went on to say that this transition might not have been easy for students who had not been exposed to modes of experiential learning. A level students needed to give up their existing values and knowledge about art and design, something that might have been quite traumatic, linked to feelings of loss and inadequacy (Robins in Addison and Burgess, 2006, pp.39–47). By applying Robins' ideas to the GCSE Applied Art and Design students it could be seen that they were in a more complex position that their older peers. They were not fully immersed into the art college as they mostly studied at school (sometimes doing courses like textiles and graphics concurrently to their college course). Using the metaphors of cleansing and purging the school students were never totally clean until they decided to come to college full time when they had left school. This had implications for how the students viewed themselves fitting into college and just as importantly how others in the college environment perceived them.

Conclusion

To conclude, it can be seen that Leeds College of Art and Design has had a particular history of teaching, using methods that are derived from the Basic Design Course and the Foundation course. The importance of this pedagogical legacy can be seen in the similar curriculum structures of the 1922 Bauhaus and the 2008 GCSE Applied Art and Design course. Tutors teaching on the course were products of this approach to education by studying on various foundation courses at local colleges. It has been argued that this approach valued the interconnectedness of subjects and fine and applied arts, and that students themselves could construct their own knowledge through experiential learning. This was explained effectively by Davie in 1959 and his words still have relevance today. Swift and Steers (1999, in Hardy, 2006) have argued that this differs from school knowledge, which was broken down into modules that were about separation rather than connectedness. Students and to some extent tutors did not control what constituted school knowledge. This did not lead to exploration and creativity.

School pupils who came into Leeds College of Art and Design one day a week were exposed to both ways of delivering art and design knowledge. Tensions may have occurred when the student has been good at art at school, but found a new teaching approach difficult and challenging. They may not have felt themselves to be a successful art and design student, that they did not fully belong at Leeds College of Art and Design, but were visitors in a strange environment. They may not have valued their own experiments and mark making because they had been praised for being good at imitation before. Learning identities were very specific to this group of students, based on coming from school but at the same time part being of the college. College tutors have become aware of the tensions students may have experienced. The implication for the delivery of art and design on the Applied GCSE was that the experiential learning model could be compromised to keep students engaged. This was done by setting many structured tasks at the beginning of the process that enabled students to feel comfortable in college before they tried more challenging modes of delivery.

Bibliography

Addison, N. and Burgess, L. (2003) *Issues in Art and Design Teaching* Oxon, RoutledgeFalmer

Ball, L. (1996) *Helping Students to Learn Independently in the Crafts: A Collection of Case Studies in Student Learning* London, The Crafts Council

Bates, M. (1968) *The Guardian 2nd July* in Leeds College of Art and Design Archives

Britzman, D. (1991), *Practice makes practice: A critical study of Learning to Teach* Albany, State University of New York Press

Cheng-Man Lau, D. (2001) *Analysing Curriculum Development Process: Three Models* in *Pedagogy, Culture and Society*, Vol. 9, No. 1, 2001 pp.29–44

Department of Education and Science (1983) *Art in Secondary Education 11–16*, London, Her Majesty's Stationery Office

Dudley, E. and Mealing, S. (2000) Becoming Designers: Education and Influence Becoming Designers: Education and Influence Exeter, Intellect Books

Goodlad, J.I. (1990) *Teachers for our Nation's Schools* San Francisco, Jossey-Bass

Hardy, T. (Ed.) (2006) *Art Education in a Postmodern World* Bristol, Intellect Books

Leeds City Art Gallery (1964*) The teaching Image Catalogue* Exhibition of Staff work 17 April to 28 May 1964

Lortie, D. (1975) *Schoolteacher: A sociological study* Chicago, University of Chicago Press

Miller, C. (Ed) (2003) *Behind the Mosaic: One Hundred Years of Art Education* Leeds, Leeds Museums and Galleries and the Authors

Schon, D. (1987), *Educating the Reflective Practitioner* presentation to the 1987 meeting of the American Educational Research Association Washington, DC. Found at. <http://educ.queensu.ca/~ar/schon87.htm>, (05/03/07)

Taylor, E. (1971) *The Artist in a Machine Age* in *The Yorkshire Post* Tuesday 23 February 1971 in Leeds College of Art and Design Archives

Taylor, E. (1967) *An Educational Idea* 25 May 1967 Leeds College of Art and Design Archives

Thorpe, M. (1993), *Culture and Process of Adult Learning* London, Routledge

The Times Educational Supplement (07/05/71) p.23, Leeds College of Art and Design Archives

Wenger, E. (1998), *Communities of Practice* Cambridge, Cambridge University Press

Wyatt-Smith, C. and Cummings, J. (2003) *Curriculum Literacies: expanding domains of literacy* in Assessment in Education Vol. 10, No. 1, March 2003, pp.47–59

Other sources

A very useful and important document from Leeds College of Art and Design Archive that demonstrated the pedagogical links with the Bauhaus philosophy was:

> Alan Davie (1959) in The Developing Process: Work in Progress Towards a New Foundation of Art Teaching developed at the department of Fine Art, Kings College, Durham University, Newcastle Upon Tyne and at Leeds College of Art, published by University of Durham 1959

This originated from an event organized by the following: Victor Pasmore, Department of Fine Art, Kings College Durham; Harry Thubron, Department of Painting and Research, Leeds College of Art; Richard Hamilton, Department of Design, Kings College Durham and Tom Hudson, Department of Basic Form, Leeds College of Art, in association with Terry Frost, Alan Davie, Hurbert Dalwood (Gregory Fellow, Leeds University) and Lawrence Goning (Professor of Fine Art, Durham University).

Acknowledgement

Many thanks for the encouragement and support in writing this paper given by Rebecca Lowe, Archivist at Leeds College of Art and Design.

Design Pedagogy and Diversity:
What are the Issues?

Kate Hatton and Sherelene Cuffe
Leeds College of Art and Design

Introduction

This paper explores issues of Design Pedagogy and Diversity in relation to a first year undergraduate elective module called Multicultural Studies which was taught to students studying a range of design courses, including textiles, visual communication, fashion and interior design programmes. We will do this by analysing our use of cultural theory concepts within this specific design pedagogy framework, noting how such an approach also led us to critique areas of the design curriculum. The paper examines issues in relation to these matters such as: how the module responded to a need; the 'Multicultural' term and its meanings; Enlightenment inheritances; design pedagogy and identity; 'fixity' and stereotyping within the design curriculum. Also noted will be the forms of presentation of theory and practice Sherelene and I used in our teaching of this particular module in order to make it successful.[1] Overall, the paper aims to relate how certain texts and concepts from the fields of multiculturalism and cultural theory aided both the teaching process we followed and the analysis we made of new pedagogic practices, in order to develop the HE curriculum in a more inclusive way.

Responding to a need

> One of the roots of the new approach to art [and design] education is the importance of considering student identity in art curriculum planning and implementation. The visual arts are expressions of people's ideas, beliefs, and attitudes that reveal the identities of individuals and groups, while at the same time, working to produce identities. (Freedman, 2003 p.15)

---

1. The background context for this paper began at Leeds College of Art and Design a few years ago with the development of an undergraduate elective module, which was given the title, 'Multicultural Studies'. This was initially written in 2002 and had at different times been delivered both by myself or Sherelene. We team taught the module one year (perhaps its most successful year) but it had normally been delivered by only one member of staff, due the organisation of staff/student teaching ratios to student groups. Sherelene's background is a mainly practice and theory based one, while mine is mainly theory based so we felt our ideas complemented each other fairly well whilst team teaching and developing the module.

The curriculum design of the Multicultural Studies elective module developed partly as a response to the Race Relations Amendment Act (2000) which made it a legal obligation for public institutions to embed anti-racist practices within their work, but it was also about developing a strategy to examine identity theory within the design curriculum. As curriculum co-ordinator for critical studies at the time of its inception, I felt there was something absent from our main programme of study and wanted to introduce a change that would also respond to the Act. By delivering a module containing an open dialogue about identity, racism and research into the cultures of design and creative practice, it appeared the institution would be offering students something they may not have had time for in their core curriculum studies. The elective also presented a challenge in the sense that a number of our students came to college without a particular background in reading or thinking around what might be called 'cultural diversity'. This was something those attending the module had revealed to us through the progress of the course.

As the ten week module developed, it emerged that the limited time period we had was certainly not enough for pursuing even a small amount of what both we and the students felt was necessary in order to further our understandings and enhance research capabilities in this subject area. Most students indicated that they felt they had only 'scratched the surface' when the elective came to an end in 2006. Nonetheless, we were constrained by such time limits on the curriculum and had to work within this framework.

Design Pedagogy and Identity

Many of the discussions we had with students in the early stages of the module reflected their social and pedagogised identities. The concept of 'pedagogised identities' is used in the context of art education by Atkinson (2002), but this idea might easily be applied to a conceptualisation of design education generally. Atkinson's theory explores how hermeneutic understandings of creativity and creative education may be conditioned by existing sources and knowledges, thus forming a specific arrangement of pedagogy and particular pedagogised identities:

> ...such identities are developed within specific discourses of practice and representation that constitute pedagogic contexts. I will therefore argue that the construction of what I call pedagogised identities arises out of valuing and legitimising particular contexts of teaching and learning experiences...I will also argue that in different contexts of teaching and learning art different pedagogised identities are formed. (Atkinson, 2002, p.4)

Some of the ideas, which supported the idea of the Multicultural Studies module, came from an awareness of the fact that particular contexts of teaching and learning had become pedagogised practices for students whose own backgrounds may have been very diverse. It was felt that this new module might allow for some reflection both by students and tutors around the values legitimised by those practices. As the teaching and learning practices evolved, the module turned out to be both experiential and developmental; its emphasis shifted and moved with the flow of the debates taking place and the research opportunities opening up to the students. To this degree it was co-constructed by the student body, although the module outcomes, containing a presentation and/or a written research paper or body of work, always remained the same.

In order to frame the idea of a reconstructed identity for one aspect of design pedagogy, which the Multicultural Studies elective was about, it might be helpful at this point to briefly examine the general nature of design pedagogy up until this point.

One might say that design (and art), education has, since the early twentieth century, followed a kind of 'psychological typology' (Atkinson, 2002), such as that which Read promoted in the fifties (Read, 1958). This was when a designer's or an artist's potential would be 'successfully' developed if he or she moved through a series of 'staged' educational practices, all of which maintained their own particular social and cultural identities. For example, it was considered that drawing must be learnt, but what types of drawing (observational, technical, representational)? And, what kinds of materials should be used to draw with (charcoal, pencil, paint, computer)? These techniques all have their own pedagogised identities based on the knowledge and experiences and possible subjectivity of the tutor teaching the subject. It is also worth noting that the assessment of such practices is also based on the success of repeating the typology.

Therefore, in this instance, the tutor would perhaps only promote those forms of drawing practice he or she is familiar with and not necessarily those he or she is unfamiliar with, which to a certain degree, is understandable. The same kind of typology is also maintained in other areas of art and design education to greater degrees perhaps within the National Curriculum. This is revealing in terms of the kinds of material theory and practice institutions expect their students to engage with and become proficient in. It would also be pertinent to note here that many art colleges have moved away from such technical origins in terms of the industrial heritages they began with, when they first appeared as Design Schools to train designers for British industry. Since then, learning by the process of making was sometimes introduced to support notions of creativity, but the impetus for doing this may have been lost due to the staged learning of the National Curriculum. New college students arrive with a particular expectation of how to work and this is very difficult for them to unlearn, even if the curriculum is broader.

This 'reproduction' of design training and particular types of theoretical meaning causes the formation of pedagogised identities which can only be disrupted if both the tutor and the student body are introduced to new fields of design thinking and new ways of culturally locating the discipline, which is a challenge both to the tutor, the institution and to the student body. If this is the case then the pedagogic field may need to be critiqued in order to dismantle its repetitive format. The example of the Multicultural Studies elective was one attempt to critique what was being repeatedly delivered to students and to introduce a new and worthwhile programme of study.

The 'Multicultural' term

It may be necessary at this juncture to explore the idea of the module title 'Multicultural Studies' as some people may think it is a little dated. Titles are important concepts as they can help construct identities. In pedagogic contexts they may also confer the ideals of the institution at a given moment in time. The use of the 'Multicultural Studies' title was itself was a difficult concept due to its fluid nature. Doy (2003) has written about the complexities around the multicultural term in relation to art history, reminding us of its necessary political nature, and suggesting we could work carefully around its use. Although as tutors deliberating over the use of this problematic term, we were probably in agreement that 'multiculturalism' may at times appear to be a part of a neo-liberal construct of 'happy clappy' multi-ethnic Britain, yet was not the political stress or aim of the course.

I have also noted in a previous text (Hatton, 2003) some of my own concerns over using the term multiculturalism, but it still seemed to me that rather than being part of a particular agenda, the term still held currency in relation to contemporary British society. Multiculturalism is also a term that most people had heard of and perhaps did not sound as complicated as 'cultural pluralism' or 'cultural diversity', both of which also have the potential to be misunderstood. In 2002, the idea of multiculturalism was still perhaps a kind of 'hopeful' critical term that the institution at the time felt was appropriate for an interdisciplinary module aimed mainly at encouraging students to study the theories surrounding their own culturally diverse society.

Further justification for using the title may be related to education theory. Some of the most advanced anti-racist educational research we have come across, from the UK and American sources, still identify with the notion of a multicultural pedagogy. Banks (2006) offers ideas on multicultural thinking in relation to schools which suggests how to achieve everyday cultures of equity within pedagogy. Ladson- Billings and Gillborn who edit *The Routledge/Falmer Reader in Multicultural Education* (2004) bring together significant theory from both sides of the Atlantic and this text demonstrates a commitment to the concept multiculturalism by using the term in its title, although the texts within this source also recognise the variety of debates surrounding multiculturalism and anti-racism in education theory. Gillborn, for example discusses how to oppose racism and remain critical within a variety of discourses:

> What is perhaps of central importance in these debates is the requirement to remain critical, not only of others, but also of our own attempts to understand and oppose racism. An examination of anti-racist policy and practice demonstrates clearly that there is no blueprint for successful anti-racism – no one 'correct' way. (Gillborn, 2000 in Ladsdon-Billings, Gillborn 2004, p.45)

In the early days of changing the curriculum structure at Leeds, the Multicultural Studies module being a part of these debates and changes, its title appeared to be acceptable at the time of writing the curriculum document. Other titles, including 'Postcolonial Studies', may have been more appropriate in some ways since our reading list gradually encompassed a fair number of postcolonial texts. Also, on occasion speakers had been invited to the institution to speak on postcolonial theory to staff and student groups. It was probably also true that some students may have been familiar with some aspects of postcolonial writing from their A level English Literature or Media Studies work, again a growing aspect of some curriculum subjects, which would have given a specialist module on Postcolonial Studies some more currency.

Nevertheless, even taking all this into account it still seemed then that the concept of a Multicultural Studies elective would go some way towards addressing aspects of the curriculum, which had not yet offered the types of reading students might be interested in and in which a broader type of cultural theory might have been introduced other than that in their core subject fields. It also signalled to first year students, of whom most would be unfamiliar with postcolonial studies, something of the nature of what could be offered as a new research opportunity, and a number of these students seemed very interested in the unit on induction to their courses. One student told me later, 'I decided there and then that there might be something for me on the course when I read about this module'. What was significant was that we found students, who attended the module in their first year, often wrote dissertations in their third year sourcing material from these earlier studies as a major part of their research. In this sense alone, it became an effective pedagogic model.

Developing the module into teaching and learning strategies: doing significant reading and research

Increasingly, it became an important part of our introductory session to examine ideas of culture and identity and to invite discussion around such things. Our introductory sessions were also designed to offer opportunities for both the student body and for us, as tutors, to reflect on the cross-curricular contexts of theory and practice and to broaden understandings of such relationships between the different design disciplines.

The first teaching session of the Multicultural Studies elective usually began with an introduction to reading and research, attempting to bring together writers on the broader aspects of cultural theory. The students were introduced to benchmark texts such as Raymond Williams' *Culture is Ordinary* (1958) Edward Said's *Culture and Imperialism* (1993), and Frantz Fanon's, *Black Skin, White Masks* (1952). Such texts were intended to allow for comparative analyses around meanings of culture, against differing geographical and cultural locations. In the aforementioned these were the locations of: Great Britain; Palestine and Martinique. Students were also encouraged to examine their perceptions of their own identities and question ideas about race and culture through reading and to bring to subsequent sessions their critical understandings, thoughts and ideas. This also worked well in opening up the opportunities for debates and the students began to reveal their thoughts on how they perceived their own cultural upbringing as well as their previous design education.

In the case of 'multicultural' understandings, whatever these might be, the students seemed to realise that their personal and pedagogic experiences mattered. One important aspect of this was about coming to terms with what their social and cultural habitus had been and how this figured in terms of their interpretations of the world around them. Often this habitus impacted on their understandings of cultural diversity. For example, some white students who came from rural areas of Britain where they had not encountered diverse groups of the population, as they might have in larger towns and cities, were often the most outspoken in terms of needing to know 'why' we needed to deliver a module on such a topic. Also on occasion, personal approaches to art and design, for example whether or not a diversity of art and design references (perhaps also looking at historical inclusions and exclusions) sometimes bore relevance as to how they also engaged with some broader design references from diverse sources. Any lack of engagement with such sources therefore, was not necessarily their fault.

Another aim of the elective was to locate a notion of culture and creativity within all art and design forms and practices, particularly contemporary work and this might include film, music, writing, fine art, fashion, textiles, interior design and communication design. Sherelene's explanation of Garifuna[2] and her cultural and creative background in the Caribbean helped a great deal in locating non-hierarchical visions of design practice. The students seemed to respond particularly well to a session when she brought in her work (see figs 1 and 2). My western cultural background in design history and theory was also explored. These approaches seemed to enable students to relax more and begin discussions about themselves. What we wanted was for them to begin to understand where to start with their research and how to do significant research.

Doing significant research also meant promoting reading. This was a good option to begin with in an interdisciplinary module as reading matters as a common research tool for all students. The reading and research was opened up by work around the resources we had brought together as teaching

---

2. Garifuna is the Carib name of the indigenous people of St Vincent and the Grenadines where Sherelene was born. It is also the name given to their language and their culture. Sherelene draws heavily from this as a source for ideas in her design work.

Fig. 1. 'Petroglyphs', Sherelene Cuffe, mixed media, 2002

Fig. 2. Detail from 'Garifuna': embroidery hanging (silk), Sherelene Cuffe, 2003

materials. The students were given a bibliography and more sources on their brief. We also introduced key concepts of cultural theory through keyword analysis, supported by PowerPoint presentations and imagery that practically demonstrated meanings. Students were then asked to individually analyse a chosen image or text using the same concept to help develop their critical and observational skills.

In addition to the Said, Fanon and Williams sources noted previously, we introduced written and visual texts by Stuart Hall, bel hooks, Bernardine Evaristo and Keith Piper. Some of these were critical sources, others literary or visual ones. A documentary film about Shonibare, (2004) whose work examines the complex issues of identity, ethnicity and history in relation to textiles, fashion and their trading empires was also shown, which opened up further discourses around both identity and the interdisciplinary nature of design, art and craft.

'Fixity' and stereotyping: a further analysis of culture and identity issues within design pedagogy

Through texts used to open up further research opportunities we had examined the themes of fixity and stereotyping. However, the concepts of fixity and stereotyping also have some connection to design pedagogy and in this paper it might be useful to make note of such things. Understanding such concepts from a postcolonial perspective, or even an anti-colonial perspective, one sees the need to draw away from cultural or racial stereotyping in terms of the individual and his or her identity. But, if applied to the design curriculum, fixity and stereotyping might also be useful perhaps to our understandings of art and design practice, in terms of examining that which is fixed or unchanging.

The work of Bhabha and Araeen, two cultural theorists, we found was appropriate in critiquing identity in terms of how fixed perceptions of culture may be challenged. Bhabha's *Location of Culture*, 1994 (especially chapter 3, 'The Other Question') and Araeen's , *A New Beginning: Beyond Postcolonial Cultural Theory and Identity Politics* (2002) were used as short texts to encourage students to make a start in their reading and conceptualising of culture and identity. These texts were socially and culturally located prior to reading beginning and students were informed they were only the views of the authors.

The notion of fixity is one, which, as Bhabha explains, is closely linked to stereotyping and the repetition of cultural constructs:

> An important part of colonial discourse is its dependence on the concept of 'fixity' in the ideological construction of otherness. Fixity, as the sign of cultural/ historical/ racial difference in the discourse of colonialism, is a paradoxical mode of representation: it connotes rigidity and an unchanging order as well as disorder, degeneracy and daemonic repetition. Likewise, the stereotype, which is its major discursive strategy, is a form of knowledge and identification that vacillates between what is always 'in place', already known, and something that must be anxiously repeated ... (Bhabha, 1994, p.66)

Araeen's writing maintains a similar polemical stance to Bhabha's in terms of cultural stereotyping, yet his refers more to the context of British art. He felt creative institutions often made similar omissions to those he found in creative practice. His curatorship of 'The Other Story' in 1989 and his editorship of *Third Text* which was launched in 1987 were attempts to remedy this situation by addressing the wide omissions from western cultural and critical theory of the theories and practices of non-western creative artists, designers and thinkers, living and working in the west.

Third Text took the position that the prevailing situation was not merely the result of human neglect or an oversight on the part of those who were involved in writing art history. It represented the very ideology of the art institution. We were encouraged in this respect by the work being done in postcolonial critical theory, particularly the writing of Edward Said. (Araeen, 2002, p.333)

Araeen's desire for British creative institutions to shift away from the Eurocentric tradition is well argued in this source. However, even twenty years after *Third Text* emerged, there are still issues around how a more diverse artistic (and in this case, more diverse design) pedagogy can emerge when many creative institutions rely on 'anxiously repeating' the already known, as he and Bhabha might have put it. The idea of reproducing pedagogic constructs and creating identities from this is to be explained a little more, further on in this paper.

Bearing the notion of omissions in mind, in the delivery of the Multicultural Studies elective, we used sources which involved studying the work of contemporary black and Asian artists and designers such as Shonibare, Ofili , Piper and Neshat. These examples offered a starting point for students who were keen to relate theory to practice. Students began developing their own archives and referencing sources from this point and began to share them as a group. The sources were not just design based but also encompassed music, literature, and other forms of cultural activities.

The traditions of design pedagogy: Enlightenment inheritances

This paper will now take a turn to look at some cultural traditions originating from the Enlightenment, which may still be adversely affecting design pedagogy to this day. This will help us to see how negative pedagogic constructs in relation to race and diversity may have been formed and repeated. The discourse below also reminds us of Bhabha's notion of fixity and stereotyping. The fundamental idea here is not just that pedagogic structures of learning can be affected by an overarching 'theory', but also how the realm of knowledge formation, conceptions of history and the making of social and creative advantage can take shape under a dominant cultural discourse.

The traditional art and design criticism one comes across often takes the line that the Enlightenment was a period of 'revelation' and 'discovery', particularly within areas of scientific and philosophical thought. However, the form these traditions took was generally patriarchal and universalising. Reading between the lines of these more formal critical histories, the Enlightenment was a contradictory period. In social and economic terms it may appear to be an era of colonial power brokering in which countries such as France and England exploited groups to ensure that the objects of classical European culture remained in the hands of the European aristocracy.

The more positive aspects of Enlightenment debates around so-called 'progress', were those which provided the contexts for aspects of contemporary thought, as in ideas about nature and the human condition, particularly if the usual religious or gendered predispositions or assumptions weren't being made. Mary Wollstoncraft's work of 1792 was one such example of this. However, the Enlightenment project as a whole still contained a gendered, racist and class based view of what constituted knowledge. Therefore, even so-called rationalist thought could be excluding, as the art education theorist Kerry Freedman explains:

> The pervasive conflicts in gender relations since the early Enlightenment may be considered
> an example of how internal contradictions in historical and cultural structures promote social

transformations while maintaining structure. While individuals were conceptualized as agents of change, the idea of natural free will contained conflicts because only certain types of people were considered 'individuals'. The struggle to destroy authoritarian institutions contained the assumption that each person was to be a free actor, implying that individuals could act on all possibilities. However, being an individual meant something different for people of different races, classes and genders. (Freedman, 1995 p.93)

In design terms, in relation to the material objects produced and consumed during the Enlightenment, it was really a period when so-called 'learned' individuals continued to embrace the European classical traditions and tastes. Taking a Grand Tour, collecting objects representing aspects of civilised behaviour (tea sets, classical Greek statues), creating libraries for scholarship and following other similar noble pursuits, appeared to be the key to one becoming informed and 'cultured'. This Eurocentric, 'rationalist' view of culture of course wasn't the only historical narrative, since many cultures and histories have remained absent.[3] The idea of an equal relationship between people did not extend to gender or race, as the continuation of the slave trade and denial of women's rights revealed. For example, the so-called 'civilising' Enlightenment project was one in which western theorists and critics routinely dismissed non-white cultural histories, as Mercer has highlighted:

> Eurocentric thought rested on the fixed assumption that Africans had no culture or civilisation worthy of the name. Philosophers such as Hume and Hegel validated such assumptions, legitimating the view that Africa was outside history in a savage and rude 'state of nature'. (Mercer, 2000, p.118)

These are ideas that Banarjii (et al., 2006) and Atkinson (2002) attempt to deconstruct further within the location of education. Enlightenment claims of self and individuality continue in post Enlightenment contexts and have been questioned by postcolonial writers such as Moore-Gilbert (2006). From such sources we can see how there has been an absence of certain voices in the context of the history of creative pedagogy, which may mean the cultural values ascribed to teaching, learning and assessment will often only be understood by those who share such values.

Enlightenment inheritances may still be found in forms of contemporary art and design practices and potentially in their pedagogies, particularly where a promotion of the self, a particular view of individuality and a conception of the creative 'genius' lies. Even where it broadens the scope of its boundaries to an international context there may still be a kind of religiosity about the idea of creative genius, as Addision may be alluding to here:

> From an intersdisciplinary perspective international, modern art has become a culturally distinct set of practices, largely conventional and institutional in form. It is realised as a range of meaning-making activities that are socially embedded, a part of the way of life is lived by a few. (Addison, 2003 p.131)

The impact of this social and cultural history can by no means be underestimated, even in terms of its impact on contemporary design education. In the literature on creative pedagogy, it is clear western Enlightenment concepts of creativity and the 'creative genius' still form the dominant canon.

---

3. A number of alternative views of design history were given at the *From Cane Field to Tea Cup* conference at the V&A Museum, London in February 2007.

The justification for using specific 'knowledges' or 'histories' is mainly that they have acquired 'landmark' status such as the Modern Movement or the 'isms' where they become, in a sense, 'classic' renditions of their particular discipline. Therefore, going back to Bhabha's concept, the embeddedness, the fixity and reproduction of concepts in art and design education, for instance in the easily repeated curriculum plans and briefs we have all stuck to year in, year out, often without questioning, we know that art and design education is still living with its western Enlightenment legacy,

Disrupting the canon

It may be further argued that within the traditions of design theory, pedagogy and practice English art and design institutions (schools, colleges and universities) have followed a canon or certain customs in terms of the production and reproduction of a particular form of design knowledge that has become by now, over-familiar. Design knowledge and its historical formation in pedagogic practice also appears to have been presented either as a technical process of learning how to draw and how to solve design problems for industry perhaps more recently related mainly to modernism and its design histories as critical sources. Such approaches, if reproduced over decades become canonical through the teaching of design curricula which contain specific forms of theoretical and technical training.

This canon copying or 'learning' from a western past as a solution to the design problem creates an emphasis on white European or white north American modernist and postmodernist industrial perspectives (some examples may include the Bauhaus, post war British design histories, or high profile designers such as Philippe Starck). It therefore presents to the student body a pedagogic vision based on the context of a western design specificity. This is not to say well known western designers are not worth studying, and that design tutors never try to dismantle some of the pedagogic structures they are faced with, but it is difficult to unlearn such relationships. Much of the opportunity for change rests with more research into pedagogic practice and a change to institutional and examination requirements. It might also be about balancing the desire to create the idea of an 'original' work, with what design can mean long term for the social and financial communities you are designing for.

There is scope for design pedagogy to explore to a greater extent such things as designing for communities, designer relationships with different societies, the use of ethnographic methods of narrative, story-telling and life history in teaching and research situations, as these work with the realities of everyday design cultures. Such approaches, together with more cohesive design philosophies which promote theoretical reflections on diverse creative practices, for example the concept of design work orientated towards local communities, or ideas around designing out of a need to recycle the materials you already have, rather than producing more, mean that students could have an opportunity to explore the self as a designer in relation to differences and diversities. Using ethnographic research approaches to aid such thinking is also a good example of how to invent the more responsive methods and approaches to design thinking and its role in various forms of society that the Multicultural Studies elective attempted to do.

There have been some helpful disruptions to the canonical approaches to creative and cultural histories traditional writers on art and design have taken. Doy's research into visual culture has opened up opportunities for the possibilities of cultural research in design contexts. She has also used an auto-ethnographic approach in one of her texts (Doy, 2005). Another good example of exploring design cultures through the ethnographic narrativitye lens, is the qualitative research project on British Asian popular culture in the north east, by Andy Bennett (2000) where he reproduces the stories of Asian youth culture and music within a local setting. By developing similar research methods, such as observation of real life situations and interviewing people living in such contexts, within design pedagogy work, would, in my view, enhance the opportunities for a wider student engagement, participation and understanding of what design and its pedagogy might mean within a multicultural society.

How do we critique areas of the curriculum to avoid repetition?

In addition to questioning the historical and pedagogic constructs design education may have been based upon, we suggest that tutors and students could also critique these by doing qualitative analysis using our own life stories, investigations of the self, and our relationships to other groups of creative people, with more reading and analysis around the issues of culture and diversity. This approach may help both the teacher and student to shift their emphases away from the pedagogised identities they themselves may have helped to develop, into a broader appreciation of design and design thinking which is more socially and culturally constructed. The Bhabha and Araeen texts are perhaps two useful starting points in such a process of critical reflection, but these sources are only a starting point. Reading more critical writers such as Hall (1997), McLeod (2000), and literary writers such as hooks (1994), Evaristo (1997), Phillips (1998, 2000) would help students further their understandings of the world of different cultures around them.

For staff who may wish to expand their awareness of design and pedagogy in relation to identity and the curriculum, Atkinson's work (2002) on art education, for example, could easily be applied to design education, and we have done this in this text in terms of using his idea of pedagogised identities. Through such a route, we might explore 'that which lies on the margins or beyond the conventions or traditions of specific formations of the symbolic order that constitutes our understanding' (Atkinson, 2002), and work towards thinking afresh about what has been at the margins of the design curriculum and make it mainstream.

Also, by exploring new forms of visual and written design texts, particularly by those who may have been 'othered', or those who may examine these ideas in their work (such as Keith Piper), the process of disrupting the past and inventing a new dialogue within design pedagogy can begin. This means such visual and written texts not only become signifiers of 'new' reading and 'new' critical discourses which might aid future curriculum planning, but they also might question student and curriculum identities in order to support critical reflection within researcher/tutor activity and therefore translate on a number of levels into an educational agency which will create change.

The significance of this paper on 'Design Pedagogy and Diversity: What are the issues?' can be summed up by the following statement which is about constructing pedagogies.

As a Black British subject with roots in the Diaspora, my sense of self is embedded in a history that is not specific to a geographical location. It draws on Europe as heavily as it draws on Africa and possibly even the Caribbean. It is the task of the educator in the 21st century to construct pedagogies that acknowledge the debt we owe to peoples from different cultures and social strata for the way we live today. If this is done all children will be placed at the centre of learning. (Dash, 2005, p.125)

If we place it in the context of design teaching, learning and assessment, surely, it asks us only to go beyond our structural and geographical boundaries to examine what diverse forms of creativity may be out there for our students to learn about.

Bibliography

Araeen, R. (2002) 'A New Beginning: Beyond Postcolonial Cultural Theory and Identity Politics' in Araeen, R., Cubitt, S., Sardar, Z. (Eds) *The Third Text Reader on Art, Culture and Theory* London, Continuum pp.333–345

Atkinson, D. (2002) *Art in Education: Identity and Practice* Dordrecht/Boston/ London, Klewer

Atkinson, D. & Dash, P. (Eds) (2005) *Social and Critical Practices in Art Education* London, Trentham Books

Araeen, R. (1989) *The Other Story: Afro Asian Artists in Post War Britain* London, Hayward Gallery

Banarjii, S., Burn A. & Buckingham D. (2006) *The Rhetorics of Creativity: A Review of the Literature* London, Arts Council/Creative Partnerships

Banks, J.A. (2006) *Culture and Education: The Selected Works of James A Banks* London/New York, Routledge

Bennett A. (2000) 'Bhangra and Asian Identity: the Role of Local Knowledge' in Bennett A, *Popular Music and Youth Culture: Music Identity and Place* London, Macmillan Chapt 5 pp.103–132

Bhabha, H. (1994) *The Location of Culture* London, Routledge

Dash P. (2005) 'Cultural Demarcation, the African Diaspora and Art Education' in Atkinson D. & Dash, P *Social and Critical Practices in Art Education* Stoke on Trent, Trentham pp.117–125 Chapt 11

Doy, G. (2000) *Black Visual Culture: Modernity and Postmodernity* London: I.B. Tauris

Doy, G. (2003) 'Reflections on Multicultural Art History' in Addison, N., Burgess, L. (Eds) *Issues in Art and Design Teaching*, London/New York, Routledge pp.199–210

Doy, G. (2005) *Picturing the Self : Changing Views of the Subject in Visual Culture* London/New York, I.B. Tauris

Edgar, A. & Sedgewick, P. (Eds) (2002) *Cultural Theory: The Key Thinkers* London, Routledge

Evaristo, B. (1997) *Lara* London, Angela Royal Publishing

Fanon, F. (1952) 'The Fact of Blackness' in Evans J, Hall S (Eds) (1999) *Visual Culture: the Reader* pp.417–420. Originally written in (1952) *Peau Noir, Masques Blancs* (1968 trans. C.L.Markmann) *Black Skin: White Masks* London, MacGibbon and Kee

Freedman, K. (2003) 'Recent shifts in US art education' in Addison N, Burgess L (Eds) *Issues in Art and Design Teaching* London/New York, RoutledgeFalmer pp.8–18

Freedman, K. (1995) 'Educational Change Within Structures of History, Culture and Discourse' in Neperud R.W. (Ed) *Context, Content and Community in Art Education: Beyond Postmodernism* New York, Teachers College Press pp.87–107

Gillborn, D. (2000) 'Anti-Racism: From Policy to Praxis' in Ladsdon-Billings, G., Gillborn, D. (Eds) (2004) *The RoutledgeFalmer Reader in Multicultural Education* London/New York , RoutledgeFalmer pp.35–48

Hall, S. (Ed) (1997) *Representation: Cultural Representations and Signifying Practices* London, Sage

Hatton, K. (2003) 'Multiculturalism : narrowing the gaps in art education' in *Race, Ethnicity and Education* Vol. 4, No. 4, December, 2003, pp.357–372

hooks, b. (1994) *Outlaw Culture: Resisting Representations* New York/London, Routledge

InIVA (Institute of International Visual Arts) www.iniva.org

McLeod, J. (2000) *Beginning Postcolonialism* Manchester, Manchester University Press

Mercer, K. (1987) 'Black hair/style politics' in Owusu, K. (Ed) (2000) *Black British Culture and Society: A Text Reader,* London, Routledge pp.111–132

Moore-Gilbert (2006) 'Western Autobiography and Colonial Discourse' in *Wasifiri* Vol. 21, No 2, July pp.9–16

Phillips, C. (1998) 'A Dream Deferred: Fifty Years of Caribbean Migration to Britain' in McLeod J (Ed) (1999) *Kunapipi: Journal of Postcolonial Writing* Vol. XX1, No 2 pp.106–118

Phillips, C. (2006) 'Necessary Journeys' in *Wasifiri Vol.* 48, No. 21, Summer pp.3–6

Read, H. (1958) *Education Through Art* London, Faber and Faber

Said, E. (1993) *Culture and Imperialism* London, Chatto and Windus

Sleeter, C.E. (1993) 'How White Teachers Construct Race' in Ladsdon-Billings, G. & Gillborn, D. (Eds) (2004) *The Routledge-Falmer Reader in Multicultural Education* London/New York , RoutledgeFalmer pp.163–178

Williams, R. (1958) 'Culture is Ordinary' in Gray A, McGuigan, J. (Eds) (1997) *Studies in Culture: An Introductory Reader* London, Arnold pp.5–14

Wollstoncraft, M. (1792) *A Vindication of the Rights of Woman* extract reprinted by Penguin Group 2004

Film/Documentary

White Tribe (1999) Channel 4 Documentary from a series on Racism, Sept–Oct 2001

The Mark of the Hand: Aubrey Williams (1990) Arts Council
Edward Said in conversation

Shonibare (2004) Illuminations

Exhibitions/ catalogues

Black Style (a touring exhibition the Multicultural Studies students visited at Bradford in 2005)

Uncomfortable Truths: Traces of the Trade Victoria and Albert Museum, London 2007 (accompanying exhibition for the 'From Cane Field to Tea Cup' conference)

Trade and Empire: Remembering Slavery, Whitworth Art Gallery, Manchester Oct–Dec 2007

Swallow Hard: The Lancaster Dinner Service, Lubaina Himid, Judges Lodges Museum, Lancaster

Boutique, The Chinese Arts Centre, Manchester, Oct–Dec 2007

Suggestions for further research

Before making curriculum changes an institution might invest in research around: the histories of design education, the relationships between designers and the design industry, cultural theory, race theory, postcolonial narratives, exhibitions and what they may exclude, global design contexts, using speakers or film/documentaries in teaching to bring cultural theorists into the institution, integrating electives like the Multicultural Studies one on a long term basis – (minimum of two years), prizes/awards for students engaged in original work, or practice/theory based research initiatives around cultural diversity, on-going staff training on anti-racism, with well established training organisations and staff/student discussions about cultural diversity in the institution.

Acknowledgement

We would like to thank Dr John McLeod, Reader in Postcolonial and Diaspora Literatures, University of Leeds for his support in our efforts to introduce postcolonial theory to the college and his lively research seminars which were delivered to students and staff.

Sustainable Design and Development:
A Personal Journey

Karen Dennis
Huddersfield University

I have always had an interest in recycling – fostered from an early age by the ever present 'useful box' sited in the hallway. This was a place where my mother would discard all the packaging and 'useless' end products of our ever increasing consumptive power and our job was to turn it into something 'useful'. This of course led to a breed of toilet roll robots and tin foil pictures. We weren't rich – my mother a clothing factory outworker and my father a newly appointed copper on the beat. There were six of us in a police house and they had married and proceeded to have kids at a very early age. These forays in the useful box thus became important opportunities for cheap play and helped foster our creativity and construction skills. They also taught me that there was a lot in the world that we didn't really seem to need but that sometimes it was fun to mould it, build with it and occasionally wear it.

As I grew, I directed my design skills towards clothing and spent my time drawing around myself on the floor to get a pattern and then hurriedly sewing in time for the weekly nights out at the local night clubs. Threads hanging off garments and misshapen concoctions didn't diminish my enthusiasm and soon a course at the London College of Fashion ensued. This was followed by a three year stint as a pattern cutter for a ladies' leather-wear company. Trips to factories in Turkey and the East End of London exposed me to the underside of fashion: the grind of the machine, the sweat of brow, the inequality but the sense of excitement, the rush of the fashion show and the realisation of a collection hitting the shops and being accepted by the buying public. It also showed me the massiveness of the industry and exposed the complex political and social tensions that existed between units of an ever-increasing global production system.

Aimed at the high end of the market, however, it became increasingly difficult for me to associate with the market and I felt my career leading me in a different direction. In the late 1980s, Oxfam called for designers for their newly developing NoLoGo[1] project and thus began an interest in recycling and the increasing realisation that the useful box of the early years had duplicated and spread over the globe. As we moved into the 1990s I decided I needed to know more and concentrated on education. As a mature student I undertook a degree in Textile Design at Leeds University, concurrently setting up the NoLoGo project in Leeds. I spent the summer in India, teaching pattern cutting, under the

---

1. NoLoGo was a project set up under the auspices of Oxfam to remodel and recycle donated garments and cloth.
We set up a workroom with industrial machinery and volunteers were encouraged to develop their design and sewing skills.

auspices of Oxfam Trading, within one of their development projects and this study later morphed into a PhD. Here I undertook fieldwork with producers in India and Nepal and saw first hand the types of problems facing marginalised workers as they fought to compete within the global marketplace. Targeted through development initiatives, these workers were seen to hold the key to sustainability and radical practices of rural development; appropriate technology, empowerment and income generation were advocated. A critique of these helped me to assess the role of textile production within the projects and to expose areas for further development.[2]

I imagine in the 1980s and 90s I was not only influenced in my research conclusions by growing environmental concerns, but also by the promise of a new social order advocated by campaigning groups, anti-Thatcher sentiment, left wing politics and the post-modern era. I had taken on board critiques of previous approaches to development and appeared to have witnessed massive inequalities and environmental degradation being created through our quest to produce and consume. It seemed that the rich were indeed getting richer whilst the poor were getting shafted. Trickle-down theories had failed and what was needed was grassroots action. It seems significant that Oxfam directed its energies towards aid within the UK and Ireland in the 1990s, signalling a realisation of the global nature of poverty and the need for action directed at its causes and effects.

As we moved into the next millennium and my PhD days were at an end, I sought to reflect further on the guidelines I had proposed in my research and sought employment within an arts and design development agency. This highlighted the mechanisms through which development was being initiated from a UK perspective and further reinforced my opinion that art and design practices could have a very positive impact on sustainable development. Three years full time lecturing in fashion orientated my thoughts around a specific design area and rekindled my love of fashion and clothing. Increasingly frustrated by a slightly narrow-minded opinion of fashion, however, and an increasing need to practice what I preached I took steps to set up a social enterprise, *Ketchup Clothes,* which I hoped would further inform my research interests and my now part-time lecturing.

This enterprise is based around the production of clothing from recycled and organic materials and, having secured funding from local development agencies, provides a good insight into the mechanisms for local development and production (images of the design work produced as a result of this enterprise are presented later in this paper).[3] In essence I suppose I am hoping that it will help me gauge the viability of eco/ethical garment production and relay both positive and negative experiences back to students. It also keeps me in the design loop, where I am forced to challenge the key issues relating to sustainable development and the important role of the design sector.

In many ways, I have felt within my research and practice a real struggle to reconcile my conflicting opinions over a sector that has its grip on so many lives, especially where it relates to use of resources, communication of ideology and practices and wanton consumerism. The design sector has enormous potential to contribute to sustainability and positive development, but so often we are presented with situations that must surely make us question the role of designers. It leaves in its wake mountains of waste and embraces many practices which fly in the face of sustainability. In many ways it must also surely make us question issues relating to inequality, exploitation and practices that rely on persuading people that they need the latest colour, shape etc. at the expense of workers' rights and the planet.

---

2. My PhD in the role of textile workers within development programmes proposed a set of guidelines and these formed the basis of my early research interests.

3. See also www.ketchupclothes.com for further images and discussion of recycling techniques.

I have also found, through the years of lecturing at degree level, a growing need to know more about sustainable development and how to relate positive practices to students of design. I still feel that recycling holds a major part in sustainable development but there also appears so much that can be done in terms of material use, production systems and questioning long-held modes of work. I have attempted to bring theories through into practice and it is reflection of this work which forms the basis of this paper. I hope that the following slightly disjointed mediations of a designer/lecturer will provoke debate into methods for talking about sustainable design, be this through reviewing relevant theory or reflecting on appropriate practices.

The Context

Sustainability as a concern for development has seeped steadily into the human consciousness over the past few decades, due to concerns over resource use, environmental degradation and the fact that, for millions on the planet, even their most basic needs are not being met despite years of concerted developmental efforts. A wealth of literature now exists concerning the application of sustainability to a range of disciplines from design, geography, engineering, sociology and politics (Burrall; 1996; Charter & Fisher, 2001; Christie & Warburton; 2001; Dresner, 2002; Kutting, 2004). At the root of many of these studies is a reflection on the words of the Bruntland Report (1987) which defined sustainable development as 'development that meets the needs of the present without compromising the ability of future generations to meet their own needs'(World Commission on Environment and Development, 1987). Inherent within this quote was the notion that addressing present day needs should not negatively impact on our ability to address needs in the future. From a design point of view this would imply that we need to look closer at the effects of our present production and consumption patterns and, where they have a negative impact, seek to address this in terms of design, resource use and production.

Sustainable development also embraces the notion that development goals should not be solely focused on economic gain but that less measurable indices such as quality of life, global equity and empowerment need to be paramount to discussions (Burrall, 1996; Datschefski, 2001). Many of these imply a necessity to consider the identification and satisfaction of the needs of development – with the poor at the root of these discussions (Chambers, 1997). Papanek, (1983); for example, in critiquing the role of advertising and the hard sell of *absolute necessities'* replacing luxuries, a result of economic development and globalisation, reflected how:

> Most things are not designed for the needs of the people but for the needs of manufacturers to sell to people. (Papanek, 1983, p.46)

He further implies that the pursuit of capitalist and industry-based policies have not impacted upon the poor. In his seminal work, *Design for the Real World* and *The Green Imperative*, Papanek put forward the idea that designers needed to reorientate their efforts around meeting the needs of the masses rather than the elite. Logically, much of this work focused on a developing world context and a reorientation of design practices around notions of appropriate technology and an involvement of the poor within design decisions.

Much of the debate over sustainability in recent years has also centred on a critique of globalisation which it is seen to place power in the hands of the few and has created unsustainable working practices (McLaren, 1998; Bell & Morse, 1999; Fischer & Ponniah, 2003). It is argued that as companies skip around the globe in search of cheaper and cheaper resources (including labour and materials) they leave in their wake fragmented communities and environmental degradation. These globalised practices also undermine local production which, it is argued, would lead to higher gains in the fight against poverty and would lead to a more indigenous development path. Attention has also been drawn to the problems associated with labour flight as more and more people quit rural areas, seeking employment in ever more populated towns and cities. Much of this labour is absorbed in the informal sector which campaigners argue offers little in the way of working rights, conditions or security. Advocates of globalisation build their assumptions of poverty alleviation on the basis that countries need foreign investment and intervention to increase economic growth and should, therefore, embrace free trade. However, opposition to this approach points to the inequalities produced through this system and the fact that the gap between the rich and poor, both in and between countries, is growing. Studies showed how the richest 10 per cent (US households) have a combined income greater than the poorest 43 per cent of the world's people (approx. 2 billion people) (Bell & Morse, 1999).

This would imply that whilst development is occurring for a select few there are still billions around the globe for whom these benefits are not being felt. Worryingly much of the power of development now also lies not in the hands of countries but in the organisation structures of corporations. For example, the World Social Forum (2005) emphasising the power of transnationalism, highlighted how:

> In terms of sheer scale of economic activity, the giant corporations now rival all but the largest countries. Comparing corporate turnover to national GNP, 51 of the world's top 100 economies are corporations... Using this measurement Walmart is bigger than Indonesia, General Motors is roughly the same size as Ireland, New Zealand and Hungary combined. (Fisher & Ponniah, 2003, p.55)

Campaigning groups, non governmental organisations (NGOs) and forums such as the World Social Forum have sought to quell the growing tide but much of the strength of these organisations knows no boundaries. Anti-global activists feel instead that there is a need to restrict some of this corporate power at all levels of local, national and international interaction and increase the power of the majority classes i.e. workers, family farmers and the small business sector. At many levels this is the result of damning critiques of neoliberal policies. Fisher and Ponniah (2003) continue stating that:

> In a world of rapid globalisation, where large corporations grow more powerful in their pursuit of economic expansion and profits, there are growing networks of concerned activists who are not dazzled by the promised land of globalisation. They are alert instead to the dangers globalisation presents to justice, cultural autonomy and the environment ... they work to make visible the damage and danger wrought by rampant and unexamined economic expansion. (Fisher & Ponniah, 2003, p.2)

The transfer of inappropriate technology, which has displaced vast swathes of labour, the promotion of westernized modes of production and the embracing of a consumer culture are also oft-cited reasons as to how inequalities, conflict and environment damage have arisen. The phenomenon of this drive to mass production and to consumption beyond our basic needs has, it is argued, led to the extraction of resources beyond the planet's capacity and studies have uncovered some disturbing facts about the future if production and consumption are to continue at their present rates. For example, predicted figures for 2050 highlight how, in order to satisfy Britain's energy (CO2), we would need just over 8 planets to sustain global consumption (McLaren et al., 1998). These thoughts are mirrored in Wagernagel and Rees's study (1996) *Our Ecological Footprint*, which states how:

> The accelerating resource consumption that has supported the rapid economic growth and the rising material standards of industrialised countries in recent decades has, at the same time, degraded the forests, soil, water, air and biodiversity of the planet. As the world becomes ecologically overloaded, conventional economic development actually becomes self destructive and impoverishing. Many scholars believe that continuing on this historical path might even put our very survival at risk. (Wagernagel & Rees, 1996, p 3)

Design Debates

Readings of sustainable development theory have thus led to a conclusion that more needs to be done to incorporate key issues into design and pedagogical practice, particularly as they relate to resource use, orientation of design and production processes and product design. As argued by Datschefski (2001):

> Most environmental problems are caused by unintentional side-effects of the manufacture, use and disposal of products. (2001, p.16)

Thankfully, steps are being taken to fully assess the product design loop and as a result, interesting research and sources of inspiration have emerged that consider an analysis of all stages of the design process, from concept through to finished piece and the environmental impact of these processes. Of key importance and relevance to designers is the Life Cycle Analysis model (LCA) which looks into resource selection, production, use and disposal of a product. It also seeks to draw into the design equation impacts on environmental, social and economic damage (Brezet & van Hemel, 1997). This approach, however, entails a closer look at our design practices and the incorporation of other disciplines and interest groups. For example, Fletcher et al. (2001) in their study of sustainable consumption in design, reflected on how:

> Lifecycle thinking necessitates a high level of design competence, intelligence and communication, supported by the involvement of new design partners such as community groups, the coming together of formal disciplines as diverse as anthropology and environmental science and bonded by the traditional, creative, organising skills embodied within design. (Fletcher et. al., 2001, p.214)

It is generally recognised that the largest impact on sustainability occurs in the use phase of a product (Laffan, T., 2003), for example in clothing it is estimated that almost 100 per cent of pollution and water consumption occurs in the use of an item due to washing (Fletcher et al., 2001). Organisations and companies have thus sought to develop a tool kit approach from which to make and inform design decisions. This includes a closer look at environmental management systems (i.e. ISO 14001), life cycle assessment, design for environment, remanufacture, environmental reporting, closed loop manufacturing process and the supply chain (Shaw, 2003). Datschefski (2001), for example, argued that products being developed should adhere to the following specifications in manufacture:

Cyclic – The product is made from compostable organic materials or from minerals that are continuously recycled in a closed loop. Solar – The product in manufacture and use consumes only renewable energy that is cyclic and safe. Safe – All releases to air, water, land or space get taken up as inputs for other systems; Efficient – 'Tomorrow will be Less' – Philippe Starck The product in manufacture and use requires 90% less materials, energy and water than products providing equivalent utility did in 1990; Social – Product manufacture and use supports basic human rights and natural justice. (Datschefski, 2001, p.5)

Addressing the issue of waste McDonough W. & Braungart, M., (2002) argued that:

To eliminate the concept of waste means to design things - products, packaging and systems – from the very beginning on the understanding that waste does not exist (p.104)

A very laudable caveat, but one that is harder to put into practice after years of relatively wasteful design solutions based on inbuilt obsolescence and fast fashion trends in manufacturing and design. Increasing environmental issues are being aligned to ethical concerns and thus sustainable design can only really be spoken about in terms of its contribution to sustainable development – be this social, economic, cultural or political.

Designing for sustainable development entails investigation into the identification of development needs with an emphasis on participatory design methods – to ensure that the products being produced are appropriate to both local and global needs. It is also aligned to ethical design in that it forces designers to reflect on production and trading issues. As such, ethical design is closely related to the power relationship within the process of design, manufacture and consumption and is most commonly expressed within terms of working conditions, wages, expectations and job satisfaction. It has been closely linked to fair trade and mainly came to the attention of the public through campaigns into coffee and bananas. This has more recently been applied to other products namely clothing and handicrafts. Ethical design also aims to redress imbalances between and within trading structures and in particular in the addressing of poverty. Ethical design also seeks to engage the consumer in the production of a given design and ultimately make them question the mechanisms through which the product came to be on the market place. Within this context, issues relating to the distribution of profits, intellectual property rights and working conditions become paramount. These issues, as it can be imagined, are very complex but are mainly concerned about ways of helping the poor to move out of poverty through trade and not aid and of making a stance against countries and companies that exploit cheap labour and bad working conditions for the sake of profit (*Labour behind the Label*, 2007).

Ethical design, however, makes a few assumptions which can present difficulties in our understanding of what makes something truly ethical. Firstly it assumes that trade and not aid is a laudable goal and secondly that the products produced as a result of this intervention contribute to sustainable development. This causes a problem in our understanding, as in how can we have an ethical china cat arguably embodying western ideals, and what significance does this production have on long held traditions and communication of ideology? Should it not also be about the relationship of the producers to the product, markets and aspirations? How can we design when we have little comprehension of what the product does?[4] I would argue this is where the fair trade lobby could do more, and especially work on reorientation towards home markets and developing tools for development that have greater meaning and relevance.

---

4. Fieldwork uncovered a woman weaving a table cloth from nettles. She owned no table, little less have an idea of why anyone would want such a thing [Dennis, 1999]

Eco design follows on from ethical design, although an environmental angle is added to the point where it is often defined as a product having limited impact to the environment in terms of emission of toxins, generation of waste and that the manufacture of any component shouldn't have a detrimental impact on our carrying capacity and sustainability. This implies that the production, consumption and disposal of the product shouldn't contribute to further environmental degradation. In many cases this would entail a major reorganisation of production and consumption practices, which in most cases have been set up to maximize profit and gain rather that to contribute to sustainable development. It also implies a closer look at the materials and technology employed.

Further design debates that have a resonance for sustainable design and development include issues relating to disposal, remanufacture and performance. Designing for disposal is greatly influenced by the debates surrounding waste and the need for biodegradability. It entails asking the designer to consider issues relating the life cycle of a product and how it and its manufacturing components may be disposed of. This thus entails a closer look at the materials used and how they may be disposed of in innovative and sustainable ways. This could be aided by product exchange, modification and modularisation. The use of biodegradable materials, for example, corn starch, and the questioning of the nature of inbuilt obsolescence can also go a long way to ensuring that the products we make and consume today are either treasured and used for their natural life or able to be disposed of safely and without threat to current and future capacity. This area draws on the work by Chapman (2005) and the challenge of developing products that are emotionally as well as technically durable. It makes us question the nature of inbuilt obsolescence and helps us critique the logic of fast fashion.

Following on from a need to ensure the safe disposal of products is perhaps the need for products to be remade as certain mechanical and aesthetic elements of a product break down or become obsolete. Interesting outcomes can achieved through taking this approach and in my experience has had the most resonance with designers and students. They are able to source materials relatively cheaply and it also makes them question the ways in which a product may have been discarded in the first place. It has also formed the basis for my own design endeavours which are described in greater detail below.

Ketchup Clothes

Increasingly in my years of teaching fashion and critical studies in a variety of HE and community institutions, I have come across students who are interested in issues relating to fair trade, sweatshops, eco design, sustainability and globalisation. On many levels it represents the general zeitgeist and popularist topics found within modern day thinking but it also seems to represent a more inquisitive student. These students wish to seek out the underlying mechanisms within which design operates and are seeking avenues through which to comment on our ever shrinking and damaged world.

At first I felt I could learn all I needed to teach these students through analysing the relevant theory and practice of sustainable design and providing analysis and discussion. However, whilst inspired by the thoughts of writers such as Schumacher, Papanek, Flectcher, Braungart and Datschefski, I felt that I needed to bring in a practical element and thus Ketchup Clothes was born. I remember being rather disgusted that my first attempt to bring this into the realm of academic discussion was dismissed with a contention that we all have hobbies. Maybe it was the fact that it was seen as 'just fashion' or maybe the fact that it wasn't a big scale project, but either way I feel it has helped me to contextualise my leanings towards sustainable design and provides a structure through which to contextualise my design decisions and outcomes.

Ketchup Clothes was essentially set up as a reaction to environmental concerns and what I saw as an ever increasing wasteful approach to clothing and objects in general. As such it seeks to explore approaches to sustainable design through the remanufacture of existing products – products that are recut to eliminate signs of wear and tear and that, for what ever reason, have been discarded by their previous owners. Set up as a social enterprise, it also seeks to explore alternative business models, particularly where this relates to participatory design, ethical production and community/social involvement. It has also been centred very much from a local perspective – local in that all resources and production mechanisms are sourced in Leeds and Leeds 6[5] in particular. At present avenues are being sought, in partnership with aNTiForm,[6] a similar enterprise, to work alongside community agencies in establishing small-scale manufacturing development initiatives.

Ketchup also grew out of a desire to explore Braungart's notion of waste and to test whether it was possible to remanufacture as if waste did not exist. Firstly this entailed an investigation into the types of products being discarded and secondly to hypothesise as to the types of products/garments these could be converted into. On a personal level this entailed forays into my own wardrobe to unearth garments bound for the charity shop and to think of potential alternatives for the raw materials contained within them. I quickly also saw these items as memory clad objects, which whilst personal to me lacked the sufficient fit or style – maybe the fabric was right but the fit was dated, in the main OK but spoilt by the occasional stain or tear etc.

On the whole I decided to focus on mundane objects – the everyday items of wear – rather than expensive vintage pieces which, though rightly having a role to play in recycling, were either too fine or expensive for my purposes. I wanted to practise democratic design which entailed the production of pieces bound for the masses rather than the elite, using objects borne through mass production rather than elitist production. The main categories this threw up were household items, such as curtains, bedding and kitchenware, old clothing, factory-offcuts and bottom drawer lengths of fabric – material bought for craft projects, never used and then part of house clearance when the owner died. To date I haven't had to purchase new fabric – it seems to find its way to me through wardrobe clearances, charity shops and donations.

The following images show a variety of recycling techniques and products that have been developed through Ketchup. These include a leather biker jacket made from old leather coats – pattern pieces were kept small to ensure minimum waste and to enable me to cut around defects (Figs 1 and 2); T-shirts cut into ribbons and knitted to produce scarves, dresses and jumpers (Fig. 3): recut jersey turned into dresses, skirts and tops (Figs 4 and 5) and dresses from old saris (Figs 6 and 7).

In many ways it is an exciting way to work – every piece of clothing/fabric presents a myriad of possibilities and there is the opportunity for customer engagement in completion of the new piece. A recent commission for a biker jacket was carried out using a customers old jacket and wardrobe surgery, where people bring in items for change, is becoming more commonplace. Pieces also have a connection to the past and have resonance with Chapman's ideas around emotionally durable design – stepping into the life cycle of a product and embedding further meaning and aesthetic/technical appeal to lengthen its life. People respond well to the individuality of the pieces and the fact that pieces can be tailored around their needs. However, it is not an easy way to work. Customer acceptance of recycled

---

5. Leeds 6 is an area of Leeds close to the University and home to many students and a large Asian population. It suffers from many issues relating to social and urban deprivation, including poverty, unemployment and lack of investment.
It has a large number of small-scale creative enterprises involved in, for example, the music industry and fashion design – operating from small studios and bedrooms.

6. See www.antiformindustries.com

Fig. 1. Leather jacket

Fig. 2. Leather jacket (back)

Fig. 3. Knitted dress

Fig. 4. Recut jersey

Fig. 5. Recut jersey

Fig. 6. Sari dresses

Fig. 7. Frill dress

products, whilst growing, is still rather limited, particularly relating to textiles, which can sometimes provoke a negative response. People make associations of a supposed previous owner and see it as a degraded product. Manufacture can be timely and therefore costly, and mass production in terms of fabric and colour can be difficult.

Conclusion

Life experience and research has led me to the conclusion that there are no easy ways of teaching or practising eco/ethical design. There exists a myriad of different approaches and in many ways it presents many more questions than answers. This is partly to do with the fact that alternative paradigms are difficult to source and research into the areas have been retardant. Luckily we are now beginning to see a rise in the incorporation of eco/ethical parameters in design practice, and theory and pedagogy and interesting case studies are emerging. The areas of development, sustainability, disposal, remake and performance appear to be useful and vital contexts for the discussion of the many associated issues and are areas that will be developed through focused training and business strategies. Ideas surrounding social enterprise also appear to have resonance with the eco/ethical design debate and it is proposed that further incorporation of this is needed within design pedagogy, be this through collaborations, targeted briefs or the establishment of key design parameters.

Bibliography

Bell, S. & Morse, S. (1999) *Sustainability Indicators: Measuring the Immeasurable* London, Earthscan Publications Ltd

Burrall, P. (1996) *Product Development and the Environment* Aldershot, Gower Publishing

Chambers, R. (1997) *Whose Reality Counts: Putting The Last First* Rugby, ITDG Publishing

Chapman, J. *Emotionally Durable Design: Objects, Experiences and Empathy* London, Earthscan Publications Ltd

Charter, M. and Tischner, U. (2001) *Sustainable solutions: developing products and services for the future* Sheffield, Greenleaf

Christie, I. & D. Warburton, (2001) *From Here to Sustainability: Politics in the Real World* London, Earthscan Publications Ltd

Datschefski, E. (2001) *The Total Beauty of Sustainable Products* Switzerland, RotoVision

Dresner, S. (2002) *The Principles Of Sustainability* London, Earthscan

Fathers, J. (2007) 'Design Education: Postcards from the Edge', Key Note Speech Design and Pedagogy Conference, Leeds College of Art and Design, Leeds

Fisher, W. & T. Ponniah (Eds) (2003), *Another World Is Possible: Popular Alternatives to Globalization at the World Social Forum* London, Zed Books

Fletcher, K, E. Dewberry & P. Goggin, (2001) 'Chapter 12. Sustainable Consumption by Design' in Cohen M. & J. Murphy, (Eds) *Exploring Sustainable Consumption: Environmental Policy and the Social Sciences* London, Pergamon, pp.213–224

Fletcher, K.T. & Goggin, P.A. (2001) The Dominant Stances on Eco-Design: A Critique *Design Issues* Vol. 17 (No. 3) pp.15–25

Kutting, G. (2004) *Globalization and the Environment: Greening Global Political Economy* Albany, State University of New York Press

Laffen, T. & Dodds, R. (2003) 'Marketing and Design Targets as Stepping Stones to More Sustainable Products' in Hon B. (Ed.) *Design and Manufacture For Sustainable Development* London, Professional Engineering Publishing

McLaren, D. (et al.) (1998) *Tomorrows World: Britain's Share in a Sustainable Future* London, Earthscan

Papanek, V. (1983) *Design for Human Scale* Berkshire, Van Nostrand Reinhold Co. Ltd

Papenaek, V. (1995) *The Green Imperative* London, Thames & Hudson

Papenek, V. (2000) *Design for the Real World,* London, Thames & Hudson

Schumacher, E.F. (1973) *Small is Beautiful: A Study of Economics as if People Mattered* London, Blond and Briggs

Shaw, M. (2003) Sustainability Principle for Product Design

UNDP, cited in UNEP (1999) *Global Environment Outlook 2000* London, Earthscan

Wackernagel, M. & W. Rees, (1996) *Our Ecological Footprint: Reducing Human Impact on the Earth* Canada, New Society Publishers

United Nations World Commission on Environment and Development (1987) *Our Common Future* Oxford: Oxford University Press

The Socially-engaged/Interventionist Artist as Educator:
Some Thoughts and Dilemmas

David Collins
Leeds College of Art and Design

Amongst other things I am an artist and an educator. My working life for the past ten years has been split fairly equally between these two roles. My aim today is to reflect on how and where these two inform and/or offer a critique of each other. Within this paper I have chosen to investigate two aspects of my artistic practice under the labels 'Intervention' and 'Socially Engaged Art Practice'. I will look at each separately, as they broadly apply to different periods of my production and tend to connect to different aspects of my teaching.

Part One – Intervention

The term 'intervention' has a long history within the creative arts where it has been used to describe a huge range of activities. For my purposes here, I will use it to refer to work which is inserted into a pre-existing environment or image with an intention to create new meanings and/or critical readings. This approach characterised most of my output during the early nineties and, in particular a body of work, I produced under the pseudonym Saatchi & Someone. These were unauthorised reworkings of commercial billboards around the Leeds and Bradford area. The first work of the series (fig. 1) was a response to a advertisement produced by the Benetton clothing company. To place it in its historical context, this was made during the five-year period when the infamous Clause 28 of the Local Government Act 1986 formed part of the law of the United Kingdom. With this clause, Margaret Thatcher's Conservative government had successfully banned local authorities and schools from 'promoting homosexuality' and they had specifically outlawed the representation of 'homosexuality as a pretended family relationship'.

These interventions were made in a largely pre-digital age where spray paint graffiti on billboards was commonplace and relatively seamless alterations like these were likely to be taken at face value by most viewers. My interest was to create believable ads with non-commercial or counter-cultural messages as a contrast to commonplace product- based adverts. Whilst the messages varied, my underlying intention was to highlight and question the narrow range of messages which dominate this form of public discourse (fig. 2).

Fig. 1.

Fig. 2.

My interventionist work as Saatchi & Someone is of particular relevance to my considerations today, as it frequently forms the basis of discussions with students. Their attention is captured for two reasons, firstly, and most superficially, the work has a veneer of renegade glamour which will always appeal to the anarchic streak in many students and, secondly, they see it as a forerunner to 'street art' and other forms of 'post-graffiti' interventionism which are extremely popular with contemporary undergraduates. Both issues place an emphasis on the unauthorised aspect of the work, which in turn raises the dilemma of how to contextualise interventionist practices in general, without either encouraging unlawful behaviour or misrepresenting the history of critical art practices and their close relationship with activism. In my own experience of Higher Education and academic conferences the legal issues of interventionist practice have generally been left undiscussed, other than where they are seen to impact on the critical position of the artwork itself. In my role as educator I mostly teach first year undergraduates and, in this context, I don't feel comfortable with such a hands-off approach. I know from my own experience that many of my 18 or 19-year-old students will already be producing interventionist work of various forms and that many more will see these methods as potentially appropriate outlets for their creativity. Given this, I believe that when students choose to work in interventionist ways they deserve support which is as robust as when they work in any other manner.

I would suggest that one clear means of signalling this is by including reference to interventionist work within briefings dealing with professional practice and health and safety. In our first term I introduce students to the broad sweep of legal responsibilities and restrictions which apply to the production, construction and display of visual communications and artworks. To illustrate the relevance of these I tell apocryphal stories of student disasters based on real experiences I've either encountered or read about in the past. These are what tend to stick in the memories of the students and with this in mind I always include at least one story which revolves around an unauthorised intervention. I want students to understand that working in interventionist ways does not absolve them of professional responsibilities. After all, a trip hazard is still a trip hazard whether it is the result of a sanctioned or renegade act.

After addressing issues of legality one must provide a frame of reference for discussions of legitimacy. If students intend to insert their work into the public realm without seeking the permission of public authorities they must expect criticism and they will need to offer some justification. This is particularly important at present, as the current vogue for street art and stencil graffiti mean students often see public intervention as an appropriate medium for any visual statement, often citing justifications such as this from Banksy:

> Any advert in a public space that gives you no choice whether you see it or not is yours. It's yours to take, re-arrange and re-use. You can do whatever you like with it. Asking for permission is like asking to keep a rock someone just threw at your head. (Banksy, 2005, p.160)

Whilst I have a great deal of sympathy for the central thrust of this argument, I worry that the suggestion that any public response is critically and morally justifiable as a legitimate form of anti-corporate activism, can be used by students as a justification for overly simplistic responses. With this in mind, I encourage students to formulate their own rationale of legitimacy rather than simply to sign up to a pre-existing manifesto. This often leads to a heightened sense of personal responsibility and a deeper understanding of their own intentions. Legitimacy can be claimed on many grounds: aesthetic, moral, or the need for an immediate response to a crisis or news story. In one instance a student of mine made an interesting claim to spiritual legitimacy. He aimed to highlight and offer alternatives to what he perceived as a spiritual crisis facing western consumerist society by inserting quiet, reflective images and texts amongst the visual cacophony of city streets.

Of course, legitimacy is also conferred by the art world itself through critical and commercial attention. During the past year we have seen Banksy's work become a hot commercial and critical property with, in one case, a house being offered for sale as a Banksy mural with house attached. MoMa in New York has recognised the significance of the street art movement with the purchase of three works by Swoon. And the Baltic in Newcastle staged a major show of Graffiti and Street Art late last year. In my own case the Saatchi & Someone series are, by the measure of critical interest, my own most legitimate works, as they have been reproduced and discussed in books, journals and dissertations far more than any of my other work (McQuiston, 1993, pp.29, 182, 183, 205; McQuiston, 1997, p.123; Poynor, 2001, p.129).

Against this background we clearly need to reference street art, intervention and graffiti within our pedagogy whilst at the same time never losing sight of the legal, ethical and social debates which accompany it.

Beyond issues of contextualisation I face the dilemmas which arise when students propose specific unauthorised interventionist works during tutorials and seminars. To help deal with this I have developed a mental checklist of questions which I take them through:

1. Why do you consider intervention appropriate and legitimate in this particular instance?

2. Is it important that your work presents itself as an unauthorised presence? Is its meaning in some way contingent upon this? If not, could you seek the appropriate permissions and execute it as 'legitimate' public art?

3. Could you present the work in the form of a proposal for action, rather than a documentation of action undertaken, a relatively simple process with the aid of digital photography and PhotoShop?

The greatest difficulties come when students ask for practical advice about how to make or install an intervention. Subsequent to a conversation I had with an artist who previously practised as a lawyer, I am very careful about the way in which I respond to questions of this nature. In line with her advice I am careful to discuss only how a hypothetical artist might approach any practical issues. I simply don't offer advice about the student's specific proposal. This simple device allows one to provide all manner of guidance and warnings without becoming too closely involved.

Once all of these stages have been passed through I finally feel able to leave the decisions about whether and how to operate in the public realm to the students themselves. They will, after all, each have their own agenda and code of ethics and, as ever, students will always manage to approach us with the unexpected. Last year one young woman for a self directed brief stated very simply that she wanted to go out and do some stencil graffiti. Her reason was remarkably simple but hard to argue against: she was fed up with all the boys doing it and she wanted to have a go to see how it felt to do it as a woman. This was a very simple but poignant observation from which she began an exploration of the practical, theoretical and political issues of working as a woman street artist.

Fig. 3.

Fig. 4.

Transitional Practice

In 1993 I began studying for an MA at Manchester Metropolitan University. My research was initially focussed on representations of masculinity and the built environment. As part of my early explorations, I made a series of interventions for the fences of building sites in Hulme, Manchester. These were simple text works which played on stereotypes of builders and the building industry (fig. 3). Whilst installing some signs reading 'Strictly Men Only', I had a conversation (fig. 4) which led to a dramatic shift in my thinking. One of the builders asked me what I was doing. I replied in line with my pre-rehearsed script that I had been asked to put up the signs by management. Another builder joined the conversation and they both told me the signs were sexist and that a woman plumber had been employed on the site only the previous week. I listened and sympathised with their concerns, whilst explaining that I was only doing as I had been instructed. I finished attaching the sign and the men returned to their work, clearly disgusted with the attitudes of the 'management'. I was surprised and fascinated by the exchange and more importantly I became very uncomfortable about continuing with the project. Reflecting on the incident later, I realized my main response was frustration that I had felt unable to enter into a prolonged discussion with the builders. I had come face-to-face with the limitations of hit-and-run intervention, and now found myself craving direct human dialogue. My instincts told me this would lead to far more interesting and nuanced works.

Initially, I tried collaborating with another artist. It was a good experience but didn't compare to the energy and possibility I had felt in those few moments with the builders. For the next two years I focused on the process of working with other people rather than on final outcomes. During this period I was fortunate enough to attend the *Littoral: New Zones for Critical Practice* conference at Salford University. This event brought together artists from across the globe who, in the words of the organisers, shared

> an interest in promoting socially engaged art practice, involvement in extended collaborations
> with community, environmental or social agencies, and little interest in centering practice on
> art world institutional careers. Much Littoral work is practitioner-led, and motivated by a sense
> of social accountability, ecological responsibility, and a concern to redefine artistic practice
> through an explorational or critical interface with communities. (Littoral, 1998)

Littoral was a seminal event for me; three days during which I discovered, and was greatly influenced by, artists and curators including: Artists Placement Group (APG), Susanne Lacy, The Harrisons, Mary Jane Jacobs, and Platform, all creating radical, groundbreaking work with social interaction as the common denominator. From that point on I adopted socially engaged art practice as an overarching label to define what I do.

In preparation for this paper I decided it might be useful to get a fresh perspective on my work, in part to see whether social engagement still seemed appropriate as a label. I asked the freelance curator Katy Rochester – with whom I worked in 2005 – what she felt was 'particular' about my practice. She narrowed it down to two things:

1. It starts from an oral process with conversation as the primary medium.

2. The final visual products are never predetermined, they are the results of the process.

I was reassured by both the simplicity and clarity of this and by its similarity to a description I use on my website:

> The work starts as a process – a large conversation – and becomes concrete through a shared desire to extend this conversation to include a wider audience. (Collins, 2004)

Part Two – Socially Engaged Art Practice

For the past twelve years I have authored art projects which centre on social engagement. The process begins with the selection of either a subject or demographic which I want to know more about. This decision is the key creative act from which all else flows. It is my fundamental autonomous act as an artist. From here I look for people to collaborate with. Sometimes I find willing co-creators immediately, but more often the search takes days of phone calls and emails.

An example of my 'subject-based' work would be *talking[bout]love*. I had been wanting to do a work about love, partly as a response against the proliferation of community arts projects focused on the promotion of safe sex. Around the same time, Prescap, a community arts organization in Preston, Lancashire, advertised for an artist to do just such a safe-sex project with disabled people, who were users of a resource centre in the town. I applied, but proposed a version where I would canvas for users who were interested to collaborate with me in an exploration of the role of love and intimacy in their lives. I made it clear my approach would not exclude frank discussions of sexual behaviour, simply that it would validate the prior behaviour of participants regardless of their sexual experience or lack of the same. I also insisted the physical outcomes should not be predetermined, with decisions about how to spent the £2,000 production budget left to the discretion of the group. Prescap accepted the proposal.

In this case the physical outcomes were a book, a website and a series of bus shelter posters in the town centre. I would characterise these as the communicative outcomes of the work, not as the work itself. By far the most significant and meaningful works were the private and undocumented conversations about love, intimacy, lust, loss and social expectations which formed the heart of the project. The only audience for these works were the participants themselves.

An example of a 'demographically-determined' project would be *openplan*, a series of works with no clear thematic link all made with the partners and employees of an advertising and PR company called Brahm in Leeds. This project included what I have come to consider one of my most successful collaborative artworks. It came directly from a conversation, and that conversation was part of a simple but structured process. Brahm have a logo (fig. 5) made up of seven coloured lines, each representing a division of the firm: advertising, marketing, design, etc. One day I visited each group of employees whose activities weren't represented by a line to talk to them about this absence and specifically to ask

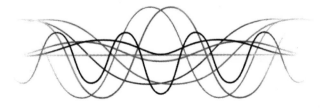

Fig. 5.

what colour they thought their line should be. The answer from one of the cleaners was 'our line would be invisible'. At first I assumed she meant simply that the cleaners felt undervalued and ignored. And whilst this formed part of her concern, far more important to her, and her colleagues, was the belief that the office workers literally had no knowledge of what the cleaners did each morning.

From this discussion, two works arose. The first, an entirely conceptual piece, is the inclusion of an invisible line within the Brahm logo itself. For me it is a permanent presence within the logo, and I hope that everyone else who has been told about its existence can also sense its presence whenever they see the company's symbol. The second involved taking photos of each desk in the building being cleaned. This was done before office hours without the knowledge of the other staff. A few days later I returned with small framed versions of each photo and the cleaners and I identified each desk and placed the appropriate image on its surface (fig. 6). We made no public announcement about this intervention, simply allowing various rumours to develop. Over time, most people realized the intervention was an artwork and, more significantly, many of the staff spoke to myself and the cleaners of their surprise about the extent of the daily cleaning, which included the careful wiping and dusting of phones, computer screens and personal effects and also carefully lifting and dusting under any papers left scattered on desks.

So how does this form of work interact with my pedagogy? When I initially show it to students, many find it hard to engage with at all, largely due to the lack of visual focus. They often enjoy anecdotes about specific projects but find no clear connection between my methods or products and their own concerns. Over time they had come recognise parallels, often approaching me for advice and support with a host of issues including: site-specific and public art, exhibition planning, community art, youth arts, documentation, funding applications and documentary-filming.

Fig. 6.

Fig. 7.

Over the years I have on several occasions involved students as volunteer facilitators and technicians in my projects. This has generally turned out well, giving them work experience and allowing me to support them beyond the confines of the college environment. There has, however, been one notable exception to this success. A few years back I was approached by a particularly strong final year student who wanted to learn more about how I conduct the conversational part of my process. Steve (not the student's real name) was a self-confident and friendly young man and I saw no reason why he shouldn't be able to do 'conversational-art' if carefully briefed. I was, at the time, talking to smokers on the staff of a large teaching hospital. I spent a few hours with Steve explaining the nature of the process and we role-played a few possible exchanges to prepare him. Despite the preparation, in practice it simply didn't work. Steve made numerous attempts to engage with smokers but became frustrated by the lack of response. During the day I rebriefed him several times but it made little difference. When we evaluated the day, two key observations emerged. Firstly, it became clear my conversational techniques were more complex than I had realised and that expecting someone else to simply duplicate them was unrealistic. Secondly, the experience made me realise the importance of my self-identification as an artist. By laying claim to the title, I am making a claim to the agency and autonomy which the role confers. By convincingly invoking the power and possibility of the artist, one can introduce a new dynamic into an otherwise prosaic scenario such as an institutional smoking room. In the role of artist's assistant/researcher, Steve simply couldn't invoke the same air of potential and possibility.

Finally, I would like to discuss a situation where my teaching impacted upon an art project rather than the other way around. *Searching for Truth* (fig. 7) was a collaboration with two young men from Chapeltown, an area of Leeds with a largely Afro-Caribbean community. The project formed part of a larger commission from BBC Radio Leeds and Leeds Metropolitan University. In practice, it began when I visited a drop-in centre in Chapeltown looking for people who might be interested in working with me. The first person I met there was called Science and he immediately told me he wanted to make documentary videos showing the 'truth' about his world. Science then introduced me to Gareth, who was also excited at the prospect. After some animated conversations about the nature of truth and the representation of inner-city and black youth, we made plans to meet up and try doing some vox-pops.

From the minute they began filming on the streets it was entirely clear to me that they had no need of my help, and that as a white, middle-class outsider I was in fact a hindrance. The potency of the process we had set in motion lay in the impact of two young, black men conducting unstructured interviews with members of their own community. Science had the forthright, but relaxed, demeanor of someone on their own patch, talking to their peers about shared experiences, whilst Gareth conveyed an air of quiet authority, laden down with a BBC-branded video and sound kit.

The ball was rolling so I left them to it. I recognized that the support they needed at this point was the same as that required by final year undergraduates. I would meet Science and Gareth every few days to debrief, review footage and plan future filming. This had the disconcerting but interesting effect of leaving me feeling that a collaborative artwork had transformed itself into a site of pure pedagogy. Without prior warning I was presented with an opportunity to act as a pedagogue, free from the constraints of the academy. So what were the differences? In practice most were superficial, we still had tutorials but they were in cafes and community centres and they didn't have any externally imposed time constraints; we had crits by inviting friends and passers by to view and comment on rough footage. The real difference came when it was time to begin editing. Science had no real interest in the technicalities of film making, and Gareth was too busy to both film and edit. I had no real choice other than to step back into the familiar role of visual facilitator which I often inhabit at the end of projects. We jointly discussed the way the films should work, I made rough edits, we all viewed and discussed these, then I re-edited in response. Science and Gareth learned about the techniques and power of editing via this process, and they continued interviewing and filming, improving their skills as they did so. Over the next few weeks we made around a dozen mini-documentaries which were shown on the BBC website (BBC, 2004) and exhibited at Leeds Met Studio Gallery. It is interesting to reflect that both young men graduated fairly quickly into new careers which built on their experiences of the project. Gareth was employed as a trainee cameraman by YTV, and then moved on to higher education. Science went in search of a media career via the increasingly predictable but highly competitive route of the Big Brother house on Channel 4. The exhibited work was also a great success, being re-shown for a further three months at Leeds City Art Gallery later that year.

Conclusions

My aims with this investigation were intentionally broad, to look for instances where my experiences as either artist or educator informed, or offered a critique of, one another. My search has been far from systematic, relying largely on a process of reviewing my notes and diaries of the past ten years as a means of recalling incidents, which might, upon re-examination, yield insight into my practice. The examples I've discussed are those which I considered most interesting and potentially enlightening for myself, and hopefully also, a broader audience. There are few obvious connections between them, although I have noticed that in most instances where a genuine or sustained connection is made between my students and my work as an artist, new and beneficial information is generated. The two clearest examples for me are: the way that by attempting to induct Steve into the role of artist's assistant I exposed nuances of my working methods that I may never have otherwise appreciated, and the way in which student interest in my work as an unauthorised interventionist opened the door to far more candid discussions about their own work as graffiti and street artists, which in turn required me to develop appropriate pedagogic tools with which to critique and support them. The experience with

Science and Gareth was of a different nature, more a confirmation that I often utilise techniques developed or learned in one field whilst working in the other – in this instance the wholesale importation of practices from one area to the other was notable, but the basic interplay occurs frequently.

I make no claims that my personal experiences suggest broader patterns of interrelation between the fields of interventionist art and art school pedagogy. However, on the evidence of my own negotiations within and between them I will certainly continue to make connections between my artistic practice and the students I teach, as in my case, at least, it seems to yield positive results.

Bibliography

Banksy, (2005) *Wall and Piece*, London, Century

McQuiston L. (1993) *Graphic Agitation*, London, Phaidon

McQuiston L. (1997) *Suffragettes to She-Devils*, London, Phaidon

Poynor R. (2001) *Obey the Giant: Life in the Image World*, London, August/Birkhauser

Websites

BBC Online (2004) *Searching For Truth*, Leeds: BBC Online
<http://www.bbc.co.uk/leeds/altogether/david_collins/truth_story.shtml> (13/03/2007)

Littoral (1998), *Littoral: New Zones for Critical Art Practice* ,UK: Littoral
<http://www.littoral.org.uk/programme_littoral.htm> (11/03/2007)

Collins D (2004) *David Collins Info, homepage*, <http://www.davidcollins.info> (10/03/2007)

Notes on Contributors

Samantha Broadhead

Samantha Broadhead is a Course leader of the Evening Access to HE and GCSE Art and Design Co-ordinator at Leeds College of Art and Design. She is also a dissertation supervisor and member of the College's Research Group. Sam's interests are around 'hard to reach' students and associated issues, such as the social and environmental aspects of learning cultures. She has published in the *Prison Service Journal* and has also taught on education programmes at the University of Leeds.

David Collins

David Collins is a visual artist with a national reputation for collaborative and interventionist practice. He works in a wide range of digital and traditional media and has been commissioned by Museum of Modern Art Oxford, IKON Gallery, First Take Films, Visual arts UK, Leeds Met University Gallery and Liverpool Visionfest. His work is generally site specific, created specifically (both physically and conceptually) for the place in which it is shown. Sites have included shopping centres, churches, buses, beaches, websites, billboards and a short TV programme. He lectures in Visual Communication and Digital Media at Leeds College of Art and Design and is a member of the College Research Group. David's present research interests include: disability arts; post-graffiti interventionist practice and the re-presentation of process-based art.

Sherelene Cuffe

Sherelene is a lecturer on the GCSE Art and Design programme and taught on the Multicultural Studies elective for BA art and design students at Leeds College of Art and Design. Her research interests have involved the work of Aubrey Williams which she has studied in the context of the following thesis: *Aubrey Williams: The Challenge to Modernism by Pre-Columbian Discourses*. In addition to her work at the college she also practices as an artist and has exhibited both in Great Britain and in the West Indies. She is a member of the College Research Group.

Karen Dennis

Currently Associate Lecturer at Huddersfield University, Dr Karen Dennis teaches specialist areas in fashion and critical studies. Karen also runs her own social enterprise, Ketchup, designing, making and selling clothes from recycled materials. Her previous posts have included Lecturer in Critical Studies, Leeds College of Art and Design; Programme Manager (BA Fashion Design Management) at Leeds University; Project Co-ordinator of Design Initiative, Manchester and designer for NoLoGo, Oxfam. Karen also helps run a community theatre collective called Pandemonium and has carried out consultancy work for ITDG, Oxfam and the German Development Service in India, Nepal and Zambia.

Gen Doy

Gen Doy is a Professor of the History and Theory of Visual Culture at De Montfort University and has previously been a guest lecturer at Leeds College of Art and Design. Her research interests are wide and interdisciplinary, and focus on the study of gender, class, race and sexuality in relation to visual culture. Her books include *Drapery: Classicism and Barbarism in Visual Culture (2002), Picturing the Self: Changing Views of the Subject in Visual Culture (2005),* and *Claude Cahun: A Sensual Politics of Photography* (2007). She is currently working on representations of migration in contemporary art.

Kate Hatton

Kate Hatton is Research Co-ordinator at Leeds College of Art and Design, the Design and Pedagogy conference 2007 and its publication being the first major events of this role. She was previously Critical and Contextual Studies Co-ordinator at Leeds College of Art for seven years and now chairs the College Research Group. Kate has two degrees in design history and is completing a Doctorate in Education at Sheffield University. Her recently published work includes: 'Fictions of the Feminine' in Peters (2006) *My Secret Rooms*, Manchester University Press; 'Multiculturalism: narrowing the gaps in art education' in *Journal of Race, Ethnicity and Education* (2003) and conference papers for: *'Diversity and the Student Experience'*, Leeds College of Art and Design, (2004) and DPR, *'Discourse, Power, Resistance'* Manchester Metropolitan University, (2006). Kate's continuing research interests include contemporary cultural theory, postcolonial studies and education theory.

Guy Julier

Guy Julier is Professor of Design and Head of Research and Research Awards Co-ordinator in the School of Architecture, Landscape and Design at Leeds Metropolitan University. He has published extensively on design issues and design culture. His works such as *The Culture of Design* (2nd revised edition, 2007) and *The Thames and Hudson Dictionary of Design Since 1900* (2nd revised edition, 2005) are now recognised as standard texts for design students on UK design programmes. An Associate Editor of the *Journal of Design and Culture*, he is also Honorary Professor at Glasgow School of Art and, in 2008, a Visiting Fellow at Otago University, New Zealand. Guy has hosted several design events in Leeds which have brought together researchers and practitioners from Europe to discuss design issues within local and global contexts.

Peter Oakley

Peter Oakley has a background of teaching and curriculum development across art, craft, design and material and visual culture ranging from KS3 to professional development for art and design teachers and lecturers. His personal research interests cover the teaching, practice and reception of art and design in industrial societies, the production and consumption of 'tourist art' made by indigenous peoples in the Southwest United States and the indigenous material culture of the Pacific Islands, together with the influence it has exerted on Western culture. He is particularly interested in issues raised by the performative aspects of craft and other creative practices. Since 2006, Peter has been part of SWLLN (Southwest Lifelong Learning Network) curriculum development team, responsible for managing projects supporting education and training in heritage construction skills, collections conservation and heritage site management and interpretation.

Janine Sykes

Janine Sykes works as a Lecturer and Co-ordinator of Critical Studies at Leeds College of Art and Design and is a member of the College Research Group. She studied degrees in the History of Art and Philosophy, and Twentieth Century Visual Culture, at Staffordshire University and she is currently undertaking an MEd in e-learning at Hull University. Her thesis on the history of art education led to a recent text tracing the history of a provincial art school which she hopes to publish this year. Other recent research interests include the development of e-learning which she developed as part of a JISC project for Wolverhampton University. In 2007, Janine also ran workshops at the staff Teaching and Learning Conference held at Leeds College of Art and Design. Future projects include seeking best practice in e-learning within specialist arts institutions.

Eleni Tracada

Eleni was born in Greece and studied life drawing and graphics at the School of Kostas Eliades, Athens, then architecture at the Faculty of Architecture, Florence, from 1974 to 1980. She is a RIBA Part III member and a member of the Society of Architectural Historians of Great Britain. After qualifying and working as a self employed architect in Florence between 1983 and 1993, she also studied MA Interior Design at Manchester Metropolitan University between 1993 and 1996 and later gained a Postgraduate Certificate in Learning and Teaching in Higher Education from the University of Leeds in 2007. Eleni taught a range of Interior Design modules at Leeds College of Art & Design where she was a member of the College Research Group. Whilst in Leeds she also participated in the Spatiality in Design research cluster; the CCASE-NET, Network for Creative collaboration in Arts, Science and Engineering, at the University of Leeds. Eleni is now a Senior Lecturer in Architecture in the School of Built Environment at the University of Derby. She also moderates and assesses the work of undergraduate and postgraduate students in Interior Architecture at the prestigious Eleni & George Vakalo' School in Athens, Greece. She is a dedicated researcher of arts, architecture and design and has published articles and papers on *Giovanni Michelucci and architecture and politics in Italy between 1922 and 1942.*

Tara Winters

Tara Winters is a Lecturer in Design at the Elam School of Fine Arts, National Institute of Creative Arts and Industries at the University of Auckland, Aotearoa, New Zealand. Her research interests include art and design education and pedagogy, design as an interface between different fields of knowledge and the shifts to more relational and responsive systems of representation offered by digital media technology. She is currently interested in research around designing a curriculum that effectively aligns learning with research and her work focuses on research based methodologies that seek to question, extend, invent and innovate as part of the construction of new knowledge for the learner. In her conference paper, teaching and learning experiences from a third year degree project in Interactive Digital Media Design are used to explore the potentials of a research driven approach to teaching and learning.